Determination of Alaska Native Status Under the Marine Mammal Protection Act

Determination of Alaska Native Status Under the Marine Mammal Protection Act

A research report
by Steve Langdon, Ph.D.

BOX OF KNOWLEDGE SERIES

SEALASKA HERITAGE INSTITUTE

Sealaska Heritage Institute (SHI) is a private nonprofit founded in 1980 to perpetuate and enhance Tlingit, Haida, and Tsimshian cultures of Southeast Alaska. Its goal is to promote cultural diversity and cross-cultural understanding through public services and events. SHI also conducts social scientific and public policy research that promotes Alaska Native arts, cultures, history, and education statewide. The institute is governed by a Board of Trustees and guided by a Council of Traditional Scholars, a Native Artist Committee, and a Southeast Regional Language Committee.

SHI's **Box of Knowledge Series** consists of essays, reports, and books that the institute considers should be made available as a contribution to studies on Tlingit, Haida, and Tsimshian cultures, history, and languages. They may be based on work carried out by researchers working in collaboration with SHI, contributions prepared by external experts, and work by staff. Publications in the Box of Knowledge Series are available through SHI's website at www.sealaskaheritage.org.

Cover photo: *A Tú* (Inside a closed container) by Tlingit/Unangax artist Nicholas Galanin of Sitka. The piece is a weathered bentwood box that features a carved wooden safe handle and carved wooden combination dial bearing the number one and fractions counting down to zero instead of numbers counting up by 10. The safe handle and combination lock represent the requirement of blood quantum as a barrier to access. Sealaska Heritage Institute Collection.

Box of Knowledge graphic by Yukie Adams.
Cover and book design by Brittany Gene.

SEALASKA HERITAGE INSTITUTE
105 S. Seward St., Suite 201
Juneau, Alaska 99801

978-1-946019-64-6

CONTENTS

List of Tables and Figures

List of Appendices

ACKNOWLEDGMENTS

This report is the result of extraordinary assistance of many people, especially Alaska Natives whose use of marine mammals is governed by the provisions of the Marine Mammal Protection Act (MMPA). I would like to acknowledge and thank all of those who were so gracious, accommodating, and supportive of this research on a topic of enormous importance and sensitivity.

I would initially like to thank Dr. Rosita Worl of the Sealaska Heritage Institute who, as chair of the Alaska Federation of Natives (AFN) Subsistence Committee, asked me to undertake research on the MMPA definition of Alaska Native. Dr. Worl and Mike Miller, chair of the Indigenous People's Council on Marine Mammals (IPCoMM), worked together to guide the research. I would like to thank both of them for their excellent insights and their responsiveness to inquiries and issues that came up during the research. I would also like to thank Dr. Worl for the Sealaska Corporation numerical data from their studies that she generously provided for utilization in this report.

Funding for the research was provided by the following Alaska Native organizations (ANOs): Afognak Native Corporation, Native Village of Afognak, Chugach Alaska Corporation, Koniag Incorporated, NANA, North Slope Borough, Sealaska Corporation, and the Sealaska Heritage Institute.

I would like to give special thanks to all the ANOs listed in Appendix 2 for allowing me to make presentations to them and to benefit from their discussion of various aspects of the issue. Without exception all of the discussions and viewpoints advanced during the presentations were thoughtful and heartfelt as the issue of future generations' use of marine mammals was of enormous significance to the participants.

Federal agency personnel of the National Marine Fisheries Service (NMFS) and the U.S. Fish and Wildlife Service (USFWS), listed in Appendix 3, were uniformly helpful and responsive in the interviews I conducted with them. Thanks to all of them.

Jolene John, Bureau of Indian Affairs (BIA) Tribal Operations Officer, was of enormous assistance in acquiring the BIA data on recent Certificate of Determination of Indian Blood (CDIB) enrollment figures that are presented and discussed in the report. She went far beyond her normal duties to both learn the database for enrollment and how to make queries for the data that I requested. She was exceptional in her assistance and I extend my profound gratitude to her for her contribution.

Carol Daniel, former AFN attorney who conducted legal research on the MMPA eligibility issue in 2010-11, was of great assistance in understanding some of the legal issues. She also provided a background file of legal research as well as important oral history on various discussions that took place on the issue in the period from 2010-2011.

Meredith Marchioni provided outstanding research assistance ferreting out the legislative hearings information about the Alaska Native Claims Settlement Act (ANCSA) definition of Alaska Native and its implementation as well as undertaking all the tabular presentations of the data that I requested. She made very important contributions to the report.

Dr. Chuck Smythe, Sealaska Heritage Institute Director of Culture and History Department, provided important commentary and editing advice on the report. Many thanks to him as well.

The report does not reflect the views of the Sealaska Heritage Institute but are those of the author alone. Any errors in the document are solely the responsibility of the author.

INTRODUCTION

The indigenous people of Alaska, known now collectively as Alaska Natives, face many complex issues in the 21st century. Some of these issues are the result of federal legislation that has defined and constrained Alaska Natives in various ways while creating institutions to address the special relationship between indigenous Alaskans and the federal government. Among the most difficult of the issues is establishing who is an Alaska Native because the term is defined differently for various purposes under federal legislation. Who is an Alaska Native, how does one know, and who decides is also critically important to establishing who is eligible to hunt marine mammals and create traditional handicrafts from marine mammal materials under the regulatory definitions of Alaska Native that have been adopted by federal agencies to implement the Marine Mammal Protection Act (MMPA). The MMPA regulatory definitions emphasize 1/4 blood quantum as the primary criteria for identifying an Alaska Native.

This report addresses issues associated with the question of defining who is an Alaska Native under the regulatory definitions of the MMPA. Topics addressed in the report include the current regulatory definition, how it is being interpreted by the agencies, how it is affecting Alaska Natives, and current views of Alaska Natives on the regulatory definition. The issue has been of great concern to numerous Alaska Native regional groups and has been the subject of discussion and organizational resolutions for nearly a decade. The report was conducted under the direction of the Sealaska Heritage Institute.

Research Objectives

The research objectives are as follows:

1. Determine the history of the definition of and criteria for "Alaska Native" to establish eligibility to hunt and process marine mammals.
2. Identify other federal definitions and criteria for "Alaska Native" that are used to determine legal rights to federal services and activities.
3. Determine if a standard of 1/4 blood quantum for activities covered by the MMPA is or could result in eligibility issues for certain populations.
4. Identify and examine alternative criteria to 1/4 blood quantum that could be proposed including but not limited to 1/8 blood quantum, tribal membership, local/regional cultural determination, descendant, and other criteria that might be identified during the research.
5. Obtain views of organizational leaders as to the suitability of alternate criteria for "Alaska Native" under MMPA.
6. Identify current circumstances in regard to enforcement of blood quantum standard on Alaska Native harvest activities of marine mammals.

Information and data acquired through research activities including documentary inquiry, interviews, presentations, and quantitative data relevant to each objective are discussed in the report. An informational and advisory handout was distributed for discussion at presentations (Appendix 1). Significant documents referred to in the report are also found in the appendices.

TRIBES, TRIBAL ENROLLMENT, TRIBES IN ALASKA, BLOOD QUANTUM

This section provides background on tribes, tribal enrollment, tribes in Alaska, and blood quantum. Each of these is a key topic with important implications that are central to the consideration of the determination of Alaska Native eligibility under the MMPA.

Tribes

Indian tribes are political entities whose existence pre-dates the formation of the United States government. Under the Constitution, Congress has the authority for regulating commerce between the United States and Indian tribes, as with foreign nations and among the states. As defined in the Constitution and in numerous federal laws, regulations, court decisions, executive orders, and federal agency policies, there is a special relationship between the US government and Indian tribes that is described as a government-to-government relationship. However, not all Indian tribes are federally recognized. The basis of this relationship is the recognition of the inherent sovereignty of Indian tribes. The Supreme Court has described the special tribal status as "domestic, dependent nations" within the United States.

The US government utilized treaties to dispossess Native Americans of their land and resources, and the government-to-government agreements created by treaties recognized specific rights, privileges, goods, and money to which tribes as political entities were entitled in return for giving up their aboriginal land. The practices of creating formal censuses and keeping lists of names of tribal members evolved following the enactment and implementation of the treaties to ensure an accurate and equitable distribution of benefits (Thornton 1997: 35). The Indian Self-Determination Act of 1975 and the Tribal Governance Act of 1990 brought about a major transformation in the relationship of the federal government to recognized tribes moving from a status equivalent to "colonial overlord" with jurisdiction over most Indian affairs to essentially a trustee over lands and resources (Parker 2016:134). In addition, the 1979 Supreme Court decision upholding the treaty rights to fisheries of the Washington tribes known as the Boldt Decision affirmed the legitimacy and continuing potency of treaty rights (Parker 2016a: 24).

Tribal Enrollment

The Bureau of Indian Affairs' legal interpretation of the Indian Reorganization Act (IRA) of 1934 affirmed the right of Indian tribes to define their own membership. The ability of Indian tribes to define their own membership has been recognized by the courts and the Bureau of Indian Affairs as a property of the inherent sovereignty of Indian tribal governments. "The courts have consistently recognized that in the absence of express legislation by Congress to the contrary, an Indian tribe has complete authority to determine all questions of its own membership" (Cohen 1942: 133 cited in Thornton 1997: 37). This principle was further confirmed by the Supreme Court in *Santa Clara Pueblo v. Martinez*, 436 U.S. 49 (1978), where the Court stated "[a] tribe's right to define its own membership for tribal purposes has long been recognized as central to its existence as an independent political community." That authority includes the right to change the requirement for membership resulting in the exclusion of members already enrolled or inclusion of those previously deemed ineligible. A recent estimate is that over 8,000 tribal members have been disenrolled in the last decade (Edmo 2016:36). It has been pointed out that the issue of disenrollment may pose difficulties for the right of tribes to define their membership as the disenrollees contest their status and bring the issue to Congress or the Supreme Court (Edmo 2016: 37). Ultimately the right of approving tribal membership criteria is under the control of the federal government either through agency, legislative, or judicial action. Definitions of Indian eligibility for federal programs and the choice to use blood quantum or not are within the authority of the federal government.

Criteria for enrollment are determined by tribal members through constitutions and ordinances. Blood quantum may or may not be used but lineal descendancy from an enrolled tribal member must almost always be established to be enrolled. Table 1 shows the position of blood quantum as a requirement of American Indian tribes circa 1997; it does not include Alaska Native tribes. The second row shows that of 21 tribes using more than 1/4 blood quantum, 85.7% are reservation-based. The last row shows the percentage of all 302 tribes (total of the three columns) that use more than 1/4, 1/4 or less and no minimum requirement. Roughly 1/3 of the tribes did not use any blood quantum whereas only about 7% used 1/4 or more. In a more recent study, Gover (2008/2009: 251) found that 70% of tribal constitutions in 2007 contained a blood quantum rule, up from 44% of tribes enacting constitutions before 1950. Tribes use either Indian blood quantum, tribal blood quantum, or a combination as enrollment criteria but the federal government does not recognize nor utilize the distinction. In regard to the discussion of the MMPA regulatory definition of Alaska Native, the criteria used by an Alaska Native tribe for enrollment may or may not be the same as the regulatory definition. For example, if Alaska Native tribes use only lineal descendancy from a tribal member as a criteria for membership, this would conflict with the current MMPA requirement of 1/4 blood quantum for eligibility to hunt and utilize marine mammals.

Table 1 Blood quantum requirements of American Indian tribes by reservation basis and size

	Blood quantum requirement		
	More than 1/4	1/4 or less	No minimum requirement
Number of tribes	21	183	98
Reservation-based	85.70%	83.10%	63.90%
Median size	1022	1096	1185
Percent of tribes	7%	60%	33%

Source: Thornton 1997; US Bureau of Indian Affairs (unpublished tribal constitutions and tribal enrollment data)

The intersection of tribal identity, family descent, criteria for tribal membership, and federal policies is a complex and controversial issue which has created many hard feelings among tribal members across the United States (Garroute 2001, Schmidt 2011). At the present time, tribes use a wide range of criteria to determine eligibility. Descendancy from an original enrollee is virtually always required. However, some tribes will accept transfers of members of other tribes who establish some relationship—residential or marital—to the tribe or a tribal member. Some tribes allow adoptions of non-Natives but legal cases that have addressed the status of non-Indians adopted by tribes have determined that such persons have not been transformed into "Indians" and therefore do not have that status before the federal government (Young 2016: 115).

The use of blood quantum as criteria for enrollment and tribal citizenship varies tremendously.

At the most restrictive end are tribal criteria that allow enrollment only for persons who can demonstrate 1/2 quantum (50%). This is the equivalent of one-full blood parent or some configuration that produces 1/2. Six tribes have been identified with this restrictive criterion. Many tribes use a 1/4 or more blood quantum, which is equivalent of one grandparent of full-blood status. Another frequently used standard is 1/8 or more blood quantum, and blood quantum of 1/16 or more is also utilized by a few tribes. Some tribes utilize tribal-specific blood quantum—for example, there may be a requirement of 1/8 quantum from members of the tribe the person is attempting to join in addition to a 1/4 quantum of total Indian blood. As indicated in Table 1, there are also many tribes that simply use a criterion of lineal descendancy from one of the originally listed tribal members found on the rolls submitted to the Bureau of Indian Affairs (BIA) at the time of formal recognition.

In addition to blood quantum and descendancy, there are a number of other criteria that can be used. A common one for reservation or village-based tribes is residency—tribal membership and eligibility for services require that the member live within the community, reservation, or defined territory. Additional criteria that have been used include language proficiency or cultural affiliation by which is typically meant that an applicant participates on a regular basis in activities (subsistence, sharing, ceremonies, etc.) characteristic of the resident Native population. Some combination of these or additional requirements that the tribe decides are important can be used as criteria for enrollment.

In the contemporary era of "self-determination," federal agencies increasingly require tribal membership in eligibility criteria for Indian programs. Federal legislation relating to Indians now almost exclusively defines Indians as members of federally recognized Indian tribes (Gover 2008/09: 244). While the federal government and the BIA continue to recognize tribes' right to determine who its citizens are, the BIA has ultimate authority over who is a tribal member since it must approve tribal constitutions. It has been pointed out by commentators that the BIA takes the position that tribes are fundamentally political entities and must continue to demonstrate that there exists a "demonstrable bilateral, political relationship between a tribe and its members." (Young 2016:114). The BIA has periodically expressed the view that "dilution" of tribal rolls by moving to lineal descendancy or other expansive criteria may cause the status of tribes in such cases to be reviewed. According to a 1988 Department of Interior Assistant Solicitor memo, the BIA could conceivably revoke federal recognition if there are a substantial number of tribal citizens who are not maintaining some sort of meaningful relationship with the tribal government (Young 2016:113).

It is critical to recognize the important distinction between individual "Indians" and "Indians" as members of tribes (O'Brien 1991). In Congressional legislation, "Indian" does not always mean "tribal member." Who is an Indian under federal law depends on various factors and circumstances as well as specific federal programs or benefits as will be discussed further below. Congress at times permits indigenous persons of the United States to benefit from Indian programs despite not being citizens of federally recognized tribes (Young 2016: 121). For example, as described below, an Indian not enrolled in a federally recognized tribe can qualify for preference in BIA hiring if he/she is 50% Indian blood quantum or greater. The final report of the American Indian Policy Review Commission in 1977 stated that as of that time the BIA had over three hundred definitions of Indian identity (Samuels 2014:144). **"Thus there is no universal definition of 'Indian' under federal law"** (Young 2016: 121).

Tribes in Alaska

Tribes were recognized in Alaska at the very moment of the transfer of jurisdiction from Russia in 1867 as the Treaty of Cession in Article III makes reference to the "uncivilized tribes" of the ceded territory. Federal governance of Alaska was assigned to the War Department, and General Henry Halleck, the Commander of the Army of the West under whose command Alaska was located, gave orders to General Jefferson Davis, the commanding officer in Alaska, to identify the leaders of indigenous groups and, if necessary, hold them accountable for the actions of members of their group (Marszalek 2004). When jurisdiction over Alaska was established by the United States government in 1867, the US Army assumed that the Indian Intercourse Act of 1834 was the guiding federal standard for dealing with the indigenous residents of Alaska. It was policy under that act that Indians were members of tribes with political organizations governed by various principles and headed by leaders. The US government claimed no jurisdiction over the internal affairs of Indian nations. Between 1867 and 1884, Army and Navy officials, as the chief governing federal officials of Alaska, gave "papers" to a number of Tlingit leaders recognizing them as "tribal leaders" and thereby holding them accountable for the actions of other members of their group as Halleck had ordered (Langdon 2013). Despite these assumptions, actions, and practices, tribes in Alaska were not formally identified by Congressional action nor dealt with under federal law. Even in the establishment of "reserves," both executive and legislative, for the benefit of indigenous groups, the term "tribe" was not used in the language creating the reserves (Case and Voluck 2015).

A critical determiner of the early uncertainty about the status of indigenous groups and "tribes" in Alaska was that in 1871 Congress halted the use of treaties as the basis of the relationship between the federal government and Indian nations. No treaties between indigenous Alaskans and the federal government were ever created. Thus treaties that have been the foundation of the relationship between American Indians and the federal government in the continental United States have not been available to Alaska Natives.

The status of indigenous Alaskans (Alaska Natives), as individuals and groups, continued to be uncertain and variously constructed in law and judicial decisions in the late 19th and early 20th centuries. It was not until 1936, with the passage of the Alaska amendment, which extended the provisions of the IRA to Alaska, that the term "tribe" was clearly established as applying in Alaska:

> For the purposes of this Act, Eskimos and other aboriginal peoples of Alaska shall be considered Indians. The term "tribe" wherever used in this Act shall be construed to refer to any Indian tribe, organized band, pueblo, or the Indians residing on one reservation.

The legislation authorized groups to organize for purposes of governance and economic development. The groups were directed to prepare and submit rolls of their members. At least 40 Alaska Native groups organized as tribes under the Alaska IRA (Case and Voluck 2015). In implementing the IRA, the Bureau of Indian Affairs developed a model constitution which was provided to tribes organizing under the IRA. In order to be recognized as federal tribes, groups had to submit their constitutions for review and acceptance along with their original roles. It is likely that some of these Alaskan IRA constitutions utilized the BIA model discussed earlier but it is not known how many.

In the Alaska Native Claims Settlement Act, the term "tribe" was used as part of the definitions of "Native village" and "Native group." The precise language is as follows:

> **(c)** "Native village" means any tribe, band, clan, group, village, community, or association in Alaska listed in sections 1610 and 1615 of this title, or which meets the requirements of this chapter, and which the Secretary determines was, on the 1970 census enumeration date (as shown by the census or other evidence satisfactory to the Secretary, who shall make findings of fact in each instance), composed of twenty-five or more Natives;
>
> **(d)** "Native group" means any tribe, band, clan, village, community, or village association of Natives in Alaska composed of less than twenty-five Natives, who comprise a majority of the residents of the locality.

Thus the existence of tribes in Alaska was also directly confirmed in ANCSA.

In 1979, the Bureau of Indian Affairs published a notice in the Federal Register listing all tribal entities recognized as eligible to receive services from the federal government because of their status as Indians. The listing did not name any tribal entities in Alaska. A subsequent list of Alaska Native tribal entities published by the BIA in 1982 was also incomplete and ambiguous since it did not include Alaska Native corporations as tribes, although they had been so designated under the Indian Self-Determination Act of 1975. Further discussion and refinement of the list continued but the issue of what were the federally recognized tribes in Alaska remained unsettled in the early 1990s. However, in 1993, the Department of Interior Solicitor's Office issued the following statement:

> For the last half century, Congress and the Department have dealt with Alaska Natives as though

> there were tribes in Alaska. The fact that the Congress and the Department may not have dealt with all Alaska Natives as tribes at all times prior to the 1930s did not preclude it from dealing with them as tribes subsequently (Sol. Op. M–36975, at 46, 47–48 (Jan. 11, 1993)).

In October 1993, a revision to the 1988 list of Alaska "entities" eligible for BIA services was issued in which 229 tribes in Alaska were listed on the federal register (US BIA1993). The list used the term "entities" in the preamble and elsewhere "to refer to and include all the various anthropological organizations, such as bands, pueblos and villages, acknowledged by the Federal Government to constitute tribes with a government-to-government relationship with the United States." A footnote defined "entities" to include "Indian tribes, bands, villages, groups, and pueblos as well as Eskimos and Aleuts" (44 FR 7235 n.1). There are a variety of names for Alaska Native tribal entities including "Native council," "tribal council," "IRA council," "village council," and "traditional council." All of these refer to the governing body of a tribe listed in the Federal Register.

It should be noted that all but three of the Alaska Native Indian tribes listed are associated with local communities, most of which are villages. Two are regional entities – the Iñupiat Community of the Arctic Slope (ICAS) and the Central Council of Tlingit and Haida Indian Tribes of Alaska (CCTHITA). The Metlakatla Indian Community is the only tribe with a reservation, which has the definitive status of "Indian Country" that provides for jurisdiction over its territory.

There are some communities that do not have tribes derived from a distinct Alaska Native village community predating ANCSA. Anchorage has the Cook Inlet Tribal Council (CITC) that has no basis in a traditional village population. Neither Palmer nor Wasilla has tribes although some Alaska Natives living in the surrounding area of the Matanuska Valley have become members of the federally-recognized Knik tribe, a Dena'ina Athabascan tribe. In Juneau, there is the Douglas Indian Association, which is traditionally associated with the Tlingit of the Taku K̲wáan. The resident tribe in the Juneau area at the time of US assumption of jurisdiction was the Áak'w K̲wáan Tlingit. The Áak'w K̲wáan are still referred to as the traditional owners of the area. While tribal "associations" are found in Seward and Valdez, they are not federally-recognized tribes.

Blood Quantum

The concept of "blood quantum" has a long history in the consideration of the status of Native American populations beginning prior to the establishment of the United States. In North America, use of the concept was begun during the period of British colonial rule (Spruhan 2006). The term references the portion of a person's genetic heritage that is presumed to come from Native American ancestors. The history of the use of the concept in the United States, by both state and federal governments, which is complicated, controversial, and contradictory, can be found in Spruhan (2006).

A variety of uses have been made of the concept in the policies of the United States primarily for the purposes of 1) categorizing members of American Indian groups and 2) determining eligibility of members of the categorized groups for benefits arising from treaties or from federal policies. Usage of concept in federal treaties has been traced to 1817 (Spruhan 2006). Common early uses of blood quantum typically took the form of 1/2 (or 50% ancestry) or 1/4 (or 25% ancestry). However, the term was often combined with criteria of 1) residency (where a person resides) and 2) cultural affinity or way of life in making determinations about eligibility. In at least one case, the term "half-breed" used in an 1830 treaty was deemed by the courts to be "intended to include all those having an admixture of *white* and Indian blood in their veins, **in whatsoever degree**" [emphasis added] (Spruhan 2006:16).

While individual tribes established relationships with the federal government through treaties in which membership criteria were typically laid out, the first Pan-Indian utilization of the blood quantum concept associated with a broad federal policy was established with the General Allotment (Dawes) Act of 1887. In order to determine eligibility for allotment, rolls (lists) were created for 167 tribes that included identified degree of Indian blood for each member but the determination was based on the mother's data only if the parents were from different tribes (Parker 2016b: 132). The BIA also instituted the practice of certifying degree of Indian blood, known as the Certificate of Determination of Indian Blood (CDIB), in conjunction with the implementation of the Dawes Act (Parker 2016b: 133). This practice was continued from 1890 to 1934 to determine eligibility for allotment from tribal lands.

When the Indian Reorganization Act (IRA) was passed in 1934, the BIA continued to use the CDIB to determine eligibility for tribal membership. The 1936 Alaska amendment to the IRA, which authorized tribal formation for indigenous Alaskans, in Section 19 stipulated that "all other persons of one-half or more Indian blood" were to be enrolled by the tribes. Despite this provision, the model constitution developed by the BIA which agents urged tribes to adopt provided that tribes should require that the parents of future members must prove that their offspring were at least 1/4 degree blood of the tribe (Parker 2016b: 133). The circular used to explain the model constitution distributed to tribes further stipulated that tribes "should limit such membership to persons who reasonably can be expected to participate in tribal relations and affairs" (Edmo 2016: 42). Tribes in Alaska and beyond have persisted in using blood quantum as a necessary evil that allows them to engage with and receive benefits from the federal government, but many are grappling with the contradiction of continued tribal viability through the exclusion of some descendants of current tribal members (Robertson 2013). Examination of one Alaska Native tribal listing of original enrollees shows that individuals of 1/4 blood quantum were included on the original roll based on the 1938 census.

It is likely that the BIA in Alaska began using a blood quantum criterion to determine eligibility for services in conjunction with the implementation of the Alaska IRA. No information was identified on how use of blood quantum by the BIA in Alaska might have changed over time. It appears that when Alaska became a state and at the time of the passage of ANCSA, the BIA was using a 1/4 blood quantum criteria to determine eligibility of Alaska Natives for services (Bassett 1971). The BIA was assigned the task of crafting the criteria for Alaska Native that was used in the act and therefore presumably brought the standard in use at that time to the definition to be used in pending ANCSA legislation.

ALASKA NATIVES AND MARINE MAMMALS

Marine mammals are an extremely important component of Alaska Native life. Table 2 is from an Alaska Department of Fish and Game (ADFG) Subsistence Division report that shows the contribution of marine mammals to Alaska Native subsistence harvests in various regions of Alaska. For rural areas, a statewide average of 18.8 kilograms (1 kilogram = 2.2 pounds) per capita of marine mammals were taken out of a total of 134 kilograms per capita. Communities in the Nome census area have the highest average per marine mammal harvest by kilogram at 102.1 per capita. At 52% of total subsistence production, communities of the North Slope Borough have the highest proportional rate of usage. No other region exceeds 20 kilograms per capita of marine mammal harvests. Products from marine mammals other than food, such as clothes for personal and familial use, are another important contribution to Alaska Native life. The sale of traditional handicrafts made with marine mammal materials provides an important economic contribution to many households and for some constitutes their primary means of obtaining cash. Rich cultural traditions of dance, song, myth, ceremony, and ritual have been created by Alaska Natives as key parts in their expression of identity, heritage, and artistic expression. The relationship between Alaska Natives and marine mammals is one of great time depth, deep emotion, and profound integration.

Table 2 Estimated harvests of wild resources for home use in Alaska by census area, region, and category, 2012.

Per capita harvest, kilograms usable weight.								
Census area	Salmon	Other fish	Shellfish	Land mammals	Marine mammals	Birds and eggs	Wild plants	All resources
Nome Census Area	29.8	21	1	30.1	**102.7**	9	9.1	202.7
North Slope Borough	3.8	11.8	0.1	54.4	**81.1**	4.3	0.4	155.9
Northwest Arctic Borough	29	78	0.1	80	**47.4**	4.5	6.2	245.2
Arctic Region Subtotal	21.4	34.8	0.5	51.7	**78.6**	6.1	5.5	198.7
Aniak Census Subarea	85	20.3	0	22.7	**0.3**	1.9	6.4	136.6
Denali Borough (portion)	39.5	5.9	1.6	13.5	**0**	1.6	1	63.1
Koyukuk-Middle Yukon	74.8	26.3	0	67.3	**0**	4.2	3	175.6
Southeast Fairbanks (portion)	21.8	12.6	0.2	51.1	**0**	1.6	4.2	91.4
Interior Region Subtotal	61.8	21.4	0.1	55.1	**0.1**	3.1	3.7	145.3
Kodiak Island Borough	25.1	27.3	5.1	10.3	**0.4**	0.4	3.3	72
Cook Inlet (portion)	59.6	20.3	6.5	16.7	**2.1**	0.8	5.2	111.1
Denali Borough (portion)	6.9	2.9	0	33.1	**0**	0.5	2.3	45.7
Chugach Census Area (portion)	35.2	14.5	1.7	22.7	**3.5**	1.1	2.7	81.3
Copper River Census Subarea	45.1	4.4	0.4	21.3	**0**	0.6	2.8	74.6

South-central Region Subtotal	43.3	11	2	21.2	**1.7**	0.8	3.2	83.3
Haines Borough	21.9	17.1	5.4	13.9	**0**	0.4	4.6	63.3
Prince of Wales/Hyder	31.4	26.5	15.4	18	**3.8**	0.6	6.4	102
Sitka Borough	26.2	24.4	12.5	23.1	**3.3**	0.3	3.2	93
Hoonah/ Angoon Census Area	31.4	45.6	14.8	27.9	**3.3**	0.5	11.5	135
Petersburg Census Area	26.1	19.3	15.7	11.2	**0.8**	0.3	2.4	75.7
Wrangell Borough	11.6	15.4	27	17.6	**0**	0.6	3.6	75.9
Yakutat Borough	66	39.5	24.6	15.3	**15.7**	1.3	12.4	174.9
Skagway Municipality	8	7	4.1	1.7	**0**	0.2	0.9	21.8
Southeast Region Subtotal	26.3	24.1	14.3	18.4	**2.6**	0.4	4.7	90.8
Aleutians East Borough	64.6	23.1	8.5	9.2	**2.2**	3.6	4.2	115.4
Aleutians West	11.7	32.8	10.2	5.4	**4.1**	0.8	4.7	69.6
Bristol Bay Borough	93.8	5.8	1.9	14.5	**4.2**	2	5.5	127.7
Dillingham Census Area	76.3	15.7	1.3	33	**5.2**	4.7	9.9	146
Lake and Peninsula Borough	121.4	16.9	4.8	38.8	**4.7**	3.3	7.4	197.3
Southwest Region Subtotal	47.4	14.7	3.6	16.1	**3.2**	2.3	5.2	92.5
Lower Kuskokwim	96.3	49.7	0	36.6	**6.2**	10.1	9.6	208.5
Kusilvak	66.9	31.8	0	34.6	**17.1**	5.1	3.9	159.4

Western Region Subtotal	86.8	43.9	0	35.9	**9.7**	8.5	7.8	192.6
Rural State Subtotal	43.4	28.1	4.5	30.4	**18.8**	3.6	5.2	134
Anchorage Municipality	4.1	1.8	0.1	1.6	**0**			7.7
Kenai Peninsula Borough (portion)	8.5	6	0.4	4.2	**0**			19.1
Matanuska-Susitna Borough (portion)	5.1	1.9	0.1	4.8	**0**			11.9
Anchorage Nonsubsistence Area Subtotal	4.9	2.4	0.1	2.6	**0**			10
Fairbanks Nonsubsistence Area 4	3.2	1.1	0	4.5	**0**			8.9
Juneau Borough	3.6	3	0.3	3	**0**			9.9
Ketchikan Gateway Borough	6	5.2	0.5	3.6	**0.1**			15.4
Valdez	9.8	3.3	0.4	6.4	**0.3**			20.3
Urban State Subtotal	4.6	2.3	0.1	3	**0**			10
STATE TOTAL	11.2	6.7	0.9	7.7	**3.2**	0.6	0.9	31.1

Source: Fall 2016: 56

HISTORY OF THE DEFINITION OF AND CRITERIA FOR "ALASKA NATIVE"

Study Objective 1. Determine the history of the definition of and criteria for "Alaska Native" to establish eligibility to hunt and process marine mammals.

What is the meaning of the term "Alaska Native"? To whom does it apply? What is the genesis of the term?

When sustained interactions with Europeans began in the 18th century, indigenous groups of the region that came to be known as Alaska were organized into families, communities, and basic sociopolitical groups. These groups were named, recognized, and identified with by their members and recognized by other similarly organized groups (Langdon 2014). The groups engaged in complex social and political interactions concerning, among other things, generally recognized geographic territories. Anthropologist Ernest Burch characterized Iñupiat sociopolitical units in northwest Alaska as "nations" (Burch 1998). In southeast Alaska, Tlingit society was organized into recognized and respected "k̲wáans" (socioterritorial units) in which clan ownership of territories was clearly and publicly established (Emmons 1990). While groups recognized linguistic and cultural affinities and differences, no broad terms for ethnolinguistic groups existed nor was the term "Alaska Native" or some synonymous term in use as no conceptualization of a defined geographic space i.e. "Alaska" existed.

During the period of Russian partial jurisdiction, from approximately 1750-1867, several broad ethnolinguistic regional terms were in common usage based on observations and characterizations by Russian observers. For example, Russian observers were aware of ethnolinguistic and sociopolitical distinctions between groups along the north Pacific Coast, such as the "Kolosh" (Tlingit), "Mednovsty" (Ahtna) and "Kenaitze" (Dena'ina). Those terminologies appear in Russian documents and charters (Black 2007). The second charter of the Russian American Company (RAC) in 1821 defined the territory under their jurisdiction to include islands south of Kamchatka and the settlement and territory in California but did not provide a cover term for indigenous populations within that territory. Distinctions among various groups were made in the charter based on their relationship to the RAC and patterns of intermarriage that resulted in persons of mixed descent appearing. Policies made for groups differed based on these variations. Thus, indigenous populations considered to be in the "employ" of the RAC had one type of policy and rights, mixed blood populations known as "Creoles" had other policies and those outside of RAC control had still other policies. The RAC charter also made a distinction among groups that were "dependent," "semi-dependent," and "independent"—a categorization that reflected social and political relations between the company and the groups. Groups regarded as completely independent were those with limited to no contact with the RAC. Thus, the RAC had no general cover term applied to populations in Russian America of variously recognized indigenous and mixed indigenous groups.

The transfer of Russian claims to jurisdiction over Alaska to the United States in 1867 was accomplished through the Treaty of Cession. In Article III that document referred to "inhabitants of the ceded territory [Alaska]" and distinguished "uncivilized native tribes" from the other residents. It further stipulated that: "The uncivilized tribes will be subject to such laws and regulations as the United States may, from time to time, adopt in regard to aboriginal tribes of that country." Thus indigenous Alaskans were equated with aboriginal tribes, i.e. Indians, found in the continental United States. However, persons of mixed parentage were implicitly lumped in the other category and deemed eligible for citizenship, presumably because they were "civilized" (Case and Voluck 2015). None of the categories or statuses utilized by the Russian American Company were brought into the Treaty of Cession although it may be interpreted that "semi-dependent" and "independent" categories were equivalent to "uncivilized."

American government officials, scientists such as William Dall, Henry Elliott and, George Davidson, and other commentators of the time following both early explorer accounts, Russian terminology, and their own observations gradually came to utilize the categories of Indian, Eskimo, and Aleut to talk about types of indigenous populations in Alaska. In the 1880s, missionary Sheldon Jackson (1880) began using the category and cover term "Alaska Native" in reference to all of the indigenous occupants of Alaska. The use of the term had two purposes. First it provided a cover term for all indigenous residents of the territory of Alaska and second it provided conceptual distance from "Indian" to facilitate the establishment of governmental policies towards indigenous Alaskans that were different from those current in the continental United States.

In the Organic Act of 1884, the ambiguous phrase "Indians or other persons" was used in regard to rights to lands in their use and occupancy or claimed by them. The Organic Act also provided for the education of Alaskan resident children "without regard to race."

Other examples of legislation and actions taken during this period concerning "Natives" include Sec. 10 of the Act of Congress approved May 14, 1898 (30 Stat. 409), which provides that "The Secretary of the Interior shall reserve for the use of the natives of Alaska suitable tracts along the water front of any stream, inlet, bay, or sea shore, for landing places for canoes and other craft used by such natives." Pursuant to the power vested in him, the Acting Secretary on Aug. 5, 1905, made a reservation of lands at the mouth of Ketchikan Creek. Similar reservations were made in several other communities, such as Juneau.

The Nelson Act of 1905 in Section 7 created a dual system of education by distinguishing between whites and "mixed race children living a civilized life" who were assigned to distinct schools. Elsewhere Section 7 stipulated that "education of the Eskimos and Indians in the district of Alaska" would continue to be carried out by the federal government. No further language concerning indigenous populations of Alaska appears in the act.

In 1906, the US Congress passed an allotment act for the "natives of Alaska" which specifically stipulated that "mixed blood" persons were "qualified" to receive lands. No further specification of "mixed blood" is provided. This may be the first precise use of the phrase "natives of Alaska" in federal law for all indigenous Alaskans. Nevertheless, it did not become a standard usage.

CHAP. 2469.—An Act Authorizing the Secretary of the Interior to allot homesteads to the natives of Alaska.

May 17, 1906.
[S. 5537.]
[Public, No. 171.]

Be it enacted by the Senate and House of Representatives of the United States of America in Congress assembled, That the Secretary of the Interior is hereby authorized and empowered, in his discretion and under such rules as he may prescribe, to allot not to exceed one hundred and sixty acres of nonmineral land in the district of Alaska to any Indian or Eskimo of full or mixed blood who resides in and is a native of said district, and who is the head of a family, or is twenty-one years of age; and the land so allotted shall be deemed the homestead of the allottee and his heirs in perpetuity, and shall be inalienable and nontaxable until otherwise provided by Congress. Any person qualified for an allotment as aforesaid shall have the preference right to secure by allotment the nonmineral land occupied by him not exceeding one hundred and sixty acres.

Alaska.
Homestead allotments to natives.
Allotments inalienable and nontaxable.
Preference rights.

Approved, May 17, 1906.

The Native Townsite Act of 1926 made provisions for the withdrawal of lands for Native communities and called for individual lots for Native residents to be surveyed and deeded. Also, there were "Native School Reserves" and "Indian Possessions" tracts marked on early plats of townsites, such as one for Haines dated 1918 (US Survey 1179). There was a survey of "Native Possessions" in the Haines Townsite (US Survey 2193, dated April 7, 1936). These were all done under the authority of the General Land Office, which later became part of Bureau of Land Management. For example, the plat of Subdivision of Native Possessions Ketchikan Townsite (US Survey 1990, 1930) was created following the Act of May 25, 1926 (Native Townsite Act).

In 1931, the Bureau of Indian Affairs was assigned responsibilities for indigenous people in Alaska taking over from the Bureau of Education. In a 1932 statement on the legal status of Alaskan indigenous populations, the Solicitor's Office used the term "these natives" four times in referencing their status as "similar to American Indians" and therefore "under the guardianship and protection of the Federal Government" (Arnold 1976:82).

In 1934, Congress passed the Indian Reorganization Act (IRA) which provided, among other things, a basis for Native Americans to organize and have federally recognized tribal governments established to conduct government-to-government relations with the federal government. Through the efforts of William L. Paul, Sr., an amendment was passed in 1936 which made the IRA applicable to Alaska. Under definitions in Section 19 of the IRA, the amendment specified that the term "Indian as used in this Act shall include all persons of Indian descent who are members of any recognized Indian tribe now under Federal jurisdiction, and all persons who are descendants of such members who were, on June 1, 1934, residing within the present boundaries of any Indian reservation, and shall further include all other persons of one-half or more Indian blood. For the purposes of this Act, Eskimos and other aboriginal peoples of Alaska shall be considered Indians." The term "Alaska Native" was not used in the Alaska IRA amendment.

In 1959, Alaska became the 49th state in the United States. Section 4 of the Statehood Act, known as the disclaimer clause, states: "As a compact with the United States said State and its people do agree and declare that they forever **disclaim all right and title** to any lands or other property not granted or confirmed to the State or its political subdivisions by or under the authority of this Act, the right or title to which is held by the United States or is subject to disposition by the United States, and to **any lands or other property, (including fishing rights), the right or title to which may be held by any Indians, Eskimos, or Aleuts (hereinafter called natives) or is held by the United States in trust for said natives; that all such lands or other property, belonging to the United States or which may belong to said natives**, shall be and remain under the absolute jurisdiction and control of the United States until disposed of under its authority…" [emphasis added]. This terminology then links three distinct indigenous ethnic peoples of Alaska—Indians, Eskimos, and Aleuts—and stipulates that they will be referred to as "natives." This language explicitly links the term "natives" to Indians, Eskimos, and

Aleuts therefore making it possible to cover them all with the term Alaska Natives. No further criteria for determining who is an Alaska Native were provided.

In 1966, the Secretary of the Interior froze Alaska state land selections under the Statehood Act in response to Native protests over state selection of important traditional territories. In 1968 federal preparation began for land claims in Alaska. The Federal Field Commission for Development and Planning in Alaska, under the jurisdiction of the Department of Interior, prepared a volume entitled "Alaska Natives and the Land" (1968). This report compiled the claims of the various regional groups to lands and waters that they considered their territory.

Alaska Native Definition in ANCSA

In 1971, the term "Alaska Native" was used in the Alaska Native Claims Settlement Act. Public Law 92-203, Sec. 3 (b) states:

> "Native" means a citizen of the United States who is a person of one-fourth degree or more Alaska Indian (including Tsimshian Indians not enrolled in the Metlakatla Indian Community) Eskimo, or Aleut blood, or combination thereof. The term includes any Natives as so defined either or both of whose adoptive parents are not Natives. It also includes, in the absence of proof of a minimum blood quantum, any citizen of the United States who is regarded as an Alaska Native by the Native village or Native group of which he claims to be a member and whose father or mother is (or, if deceased, was) regarded as Native by any village or group.

The reasoning behind the language used in the ANCSA definition of "Native" was not identified through extensive internet, periodical, or government document searches.

There are several important considerations about this definition. It introduces a "blood quantum" criterion of "one-fourth degree or more" for eligibility. It excludes Tsimshians who are enrolled with the Metlakatla Indian Community. It also includes language that makes alternative determinations of Alaska Native status possible "in the absence of proof of a minimum blood quantum…" Definitions are also provided for the terms "Native village or Native group," which are referred to as part of the alternative determination.

The language of "blood quantum" as well as the specified level of 1/4 appears to be based on federal regulations and BIA definitions establishing the criteria for American Indian that were the common practice of the federal government at the time of the passage of ANCSA. Alaska Natives were not formally consulted concerning the use of "blood quantum" as enrollment criteria. Alaska Natives who were members of IRA tribes may have become familiar with the requirement but it is likely that most Alaska Natives were unfamiliar with the concept and federal laws and policies linked to the concept.

A number of Alaska Native leaders at the time recognized that proving 1/4 blood quantum through birth certificates would likely be a problem for many Alaska Natives, especially in the Koniag and Aleut regions. Paul Ongtooguk (www.alaskool.org/projects/ancsa/annancsa accessed May 21, 2016) has written that the subsection stating "in the absence of proof of a minimum blood quantum…" was a result of an initiative made by Flore Lekanof. Lekanof was a major Aleut leader who wanted to ensure the Aleut people would qualify for ANCSA benefits. Lekanof reminded people during the ANCSA meetings and discussion with Congressional staff that Russian and European settlers had resided in the Aleutians for more than 200 years and during that time they intermarried with Aleut families. The "In the absence of proof of minimum blood quantum…" language became known as the "Aleut provision," as it allowed for Aleut and other Alaska Native peoples to be deemed Native in the absence of one quarter blood quantum (Ongtooguk: www.alaskool.org/projects/ancsa/annancsa accessed May 21, 2016). Koniag Elder and leader Perry Eaton suggested that his father, Hank Eaton, Cecil Barnes (Chugach), and John Borbridge (Sealaska) in addition to Flore Lekanof participated in the lobbying effort to ensure that there would be a way for Alaska Natives to be enrolled who were not able to find satisfactory paperwork (birth certificates) to demonstrate 1/4 blood quantum (Eaton personal communication, July 12, 2016). This language benefited not only Aleuts, but many other Alaska Natives who otherwise would have been excluded from ANCSA (Ongtooguk: www.alaskool.org/projects/ancsa/annancsa accessed July 31, 2016).

Senator Ernest Gruening made the following observation concerning the use of blood quantum and the level it was set at during deliberations on the act. Senator Gruening replied to questioning from attorney Edgar Paul Boyko in Senate hearings Feb. 8-10, 1968, as follows:

> Mr. Flore Lekanof raised the point that he thought it was unfair to limit this to Natives that were one-quarter blood and that it should be raised to one-eighth. I would like to see that blood provisions entirely eliminated. I think it will lead us down all kinds of alleys… I feel that we should have a provision that anybody who is considered a Native by his people, who has lived in the Native community, who has been a Native, should be included. (Hearings before the Committee on Interior and Insular Affairs United States Senate on S. 2906, Feb. 8-10, 1968, page 334)

The "regarded as" provision in ANCSA, in Gruening's view, was to allow those who lived in a Native community and who were considered Native to be enrolled. He clearly was also concerned about the impacts of blood quantum as a standard in general but also at the 1/4 level. The specific language was included to make sure that Alaska Natives who were regarded as Natives but for whatever reason could not demonstrate 1/4 blood quantum would be able to be enrolled.

The ANCSA enrollment process was grueling, uneven, and fraught with difficulties. "Through an all-out effort by the regional associations and Bureau of Indian Affairs (BIA) personnel, th[e] deadline was met—but at the expense of thoroughness and accuracy" (ESG 1985: III-3). Due to budgetary shortfall, the Enrollment Office was forced to contract with regional associations to assist with enrollment. Personnel from these organizations traveled to Alaska Native communities and endeavored to accurately enroll all Alaska Natives. They discovered that many Alaska Natives had difficulties filling out the "family tree" form, providing the necessary birth certificates, or obtaining affidavits from community residents verifying their status as Natives (ESG 1985: III-4). BIA Tribal Operations Officer Jolene John (personal communication, July 8, 2016) stated that those doing the enrollments exercised their "best judgment" in regard to the Native status of persons with whom they were dealing.

The problem of obtaining birth certificates and other records that demonstrated 1/4 Alaska Native blood quantum was especially troublesome in the Koniag region. There were a number of reasons including loss and fires that destroyed genealogical papers of many families. In addition, there was substantial stigma associated with being identified as Alaska Native. Koniag Elder Perry Eaton (personal communication, July 12, 2016) commented that at the time, being served by the Indian Health Service required that a person be 1/8 Alaska Native blood quantum so this was the level that people would report even if they were considerably higher. Individuals of mixed identities tended to emphasize their Caucasian heritage and suppress their Alaska Native heritage in order to escape the stigma of Alaska Native status that was held by Caucasians at the time.

Eaton (personal communication, July 12, 2016) further recalled that in Kodiak city, Nancy Anderson, then the executive director of the Kodiak Village tribe, sent a letter to the ANCSA enrollment office listing 15 names of persons who should be enrolled as they were "regarded as Alaska Natives" by the village as had been at least one of their parents. She asserted that named individuals were of similar status to Perry Eaton, who had already been enrolled. Soon after, Eaton indicated that he received a letter from ANCSA enrollment challenging his eligibility. This was at a time when he had already been enrolled and was serving on the Koniag board of directors. He then obtained letters from the Kodiak village tribe, Koniag Inc., and the village of Ouzinkie all testifying that he was "regarded as an Alaska Native" by those entities. He submitted the letters to the ANCSA enrollment office and subsequently received a letter notifying him that he had been enrolled. He was not aware of the names of others in the letter Anderson sent and was not aware of how they were regarded by the ANCSA enrollment office. Eaton (personal communication, July 12, 2016) also noted that he was aware that a prospective Sealaska shareholder had received a letter advising him of pending disenrollment like the one he had received. Although it is not clear what steps were taken by Sealaska to address the matter, the person was subsequently enrolled as a Sealaska shareholder (Worl personal communication, July 18, 2016).

As noted by Worl (personal communication, July 27, 2016) through ANCSA, with its adoption of corporations and shareholder status, the federal government created a new federal identity for indigenous people which carries with it distinct legal characteristics for certain purposes and a unique legal status as shareholders.

Marine Mammal Protection Act Definition of Alaska Native – Statute and Regulations

On October 21, 1972, Congress enacted the Marine Mammal Protection Act (MMPA) to prohibit the "take" of certain marine mammal species with special attention to those in danger of depletion or extinction. Through the efforts of then Alaska Senator Ted Stevens, Section 101(b) provides an "exemption" that allows Alaska Natives to take marine mammals for subsistence purposes and/or for the creating and selling of authentic Native articles of handicrafts and clothing. The MMPA defines an Alaska Native as:

> … any Indian, Aleut, or Eskimo who resides in Alaska and who dwells on the coast of the North Pacific Ocean or the Arctic…

The statute has no definition of "Indian, Aleut, or Eskimo." Laws passed by Congress are subsequently accompanied by regulations generally developed by the agencies charged with implementing and enforcing the law. The United States Code of Federal Regulations CFR 50 provides these implementing regulations for the MMPA. Title 50 is the principal set of rules, regulations, and definitions issued by federal agencies of the United States regarding wildlife and fisheries. Regulations regarding the Marine Mammal Protection Act are included within Title 50. The original date of MMPA regulations publication is Feb. 25, 1974.

The definition of "Alaskan Native" in the CFR Title 50 by USFWS and NOAA was modeled on the ANCSA definition in its major provisions. Nevertheless, there are several differences between the ANCSA and MMPA regulatory definitions that are discussed below.

The US Fish and Wildlife Service current regulation (50 CFR § 18.3) reads as follows:

> *Alaskan Native* means a person defined in the Alaska Native Claims Settlement Act (43 U.S.C. section 1603(b) (85 Stat. 588)) as a citizen of the United States who is of one-fourth degree or more Alaska Indian (including Tsimshian Indians enrolled or not enrolled in the Metlaktla [sic] Indian Community), Eskimo, or Aleut blood, or combination thereof. The term includes any Native, as so defined, either or both of whose adoptive parents are not Natives. It also includes, in the absence of proof of a minimum blood quantum, any citizen of the United States who is regarded as an Alaska Native by the Native village or town of which he claims to be a member and whose

> father or mother is (or, if deceased, was) regarded as Native by any Native village or Native town. Any citizen enrolled by the Secretary pursuant to section 5 of the Alaska Native Claims Settlement Act shall be conclusively presumed to be an Alaskan Native for purposes of this part.

The National Oceanic and Atmospheric Administration current regulation (50 CFR § 216.3) reads as follows:

> *Alaskan Native* means a person defined in the Alaska Native Claims Settlement Act (43 U.S.C. 1602(b)) (85 Stat. 588) as a citizen of the United States who is of one-fourth degree or more Alaska Indian (including Tsimishian [sic] Indians enrolled or not enrolled in the Metlaktla [sic] Indian Community), Eskimo, or Aleut blood or combination thereof. The term includes any Native, as so defined, either or both of whose adoptive parents are not Natives. It also includes, in the absence of proof of a minimum blood quantum, any citizen of the United States who is regarded as an Alaska Native by the Native village or group, of which he claims to be a member and whose father or mother is (or, if deceased, was) regarded as Native by any Native village or Native group. Any such citizen enrolled by the Secretary of the Interior pursuant to section 5 of the Alaska Native Claims Settlement Act shall be conclusively presumed to be an Alaskan Native for purposes of this part.

The reason for the agencies' separate regulatory definitions is that they have jurisdiction over different marine mammals and are required to publish regulations separately. USFWS is responsible for polar bears, sea otters, and walrus. NOAA is responsible for whales (bowhead, beluga, gray), seals (fur, harbor, bearded, ringed, spotted), and sea lions.

The only difference in language between the two agency regulations is the use of the term "town" twice in the USFWS definition whereas the word "group" rather than "town" is used twice in the NOAA definition. The term "group" is used in ANCSA but not "town."

Significance of Differences between ANCSA and MMPA Regulatory Definitions of Alaska Native

While the MMPA regulatory definitions of Alaska Native and the criteria for determination are modeled on the ANCSA definition, there are two differences of note. First, the MMPA definition includes Tsimshian enrolled members of the Metlakatla community who were excluded from the ANCSA definition. Second, the MMPA regulatory definition in the last sentence stipulates that Alaska Natives enrolled under ANCSA Section 5 (original) are "conclusively presumed to be an Alaska Native..."

The language stating that persons enrolled under ANCSA Section 5 are deemed eligible is significant in two ways. First, this section deals with the establishment of the initial ANCSA shareholder enrollment. This creates a distinct legal cohort of persons. Alaska Native lineal descendants of original enrollees who have inherited initial issue stock would not be considered eligible for the MMPA exemption under this language on that basis alone as they are not members of the original ANCSA shareholder cohort. Alaska Native lineal descendant inheritors of stock from original enrollees would not meet the MMPA definition unless they too were of 1/4 blood quantum.

"Descendant" was defined by amendment in ANCSA Section 3 (43 U.S.C. 1602) by amendment in 1988 to mean: "(1) a lineal descendant of a Native or of an individual who would have been a Native if such individual were alive on December 18, 1971, or (2) an adoptee of a Native or of a descendant of a Native, whose adoption (A) occurred prior to his or her majority, and (B) is recognized at law or in equity." The second ANCSA descendant definition does not include a blood quantum requirement but also recognizes non-Alaska Native adoptees of Alaska Natives as defined in ANCSA originally as lineal descendants. Second, amendments to ANCSA in 1988 allowing for enrollment of new shareholders was placed in Section 7. Alaska Natives who enrolled under the provisions for new shareholders passed in 1988 therefore would almost certainly not be eligible under the MMPA due to the fact that they enrolled under provisions of Section 7. Subsection (g) of Section 7 (43 U.S.C. 1606(g)) was amended to allow for admittance of shareholders holding new classes of stock. Original ANCSA shareholders received their stock through provisions in Section 5 (Daniels 2010).

Summation

The term "Alaska Native" is a construction arising out of the needs of the government of the United States to have a term to cover the indigenous ethnolinguistic groups of the territory of Alaska, two of which (Eskimos and Aleuts) were not classified as "Indian." Until the middle of the 20th century, various different definitions for the indigenous population of Alaska were used. In some definitions, persons of mixed ancestry were included. The term "Alaska Native" was not stabilized in federal usage and policy until the second half of the 20th century. ANCSA, the unique settlement of indigenous land claims in Alaska, established a new federal identity for indigenous people in Alaska associated with the status of Alaska Native corporation shareholder. The definition of Alaska Native that appears in ANCSA utilizing blood quantum was apparently derived from BIA definitions for Indians used in the continental United States at that time. The additional language allowing for means of enrollment other than blood quantum was included in recognition that establishing blood quantum eligibility might be difficult for many Alaska Natives and that being "regarded as" a Native by members of the community in which one resided was a more definitive testament to Nativeness than blood quantum.

OTHER DEFINITIONS OF "ALASKA NATIVE" IN PRESENT USE

Study Objective 2. Identify other federal definitions and criteria for "Alaska Native" that are used to determine legal rights to federal services and activities.

This section presents information on various ways in which "Alaska Native" has been defined recently by federal agencies and Alaska Native regional corporations. The two most important definitions of "Alaska Native" for most Alaska Natives receiving federal services are those of the Bureau of Indian Affairs (BIA) and the Indian Health Service (IHS). There are many other definitions for "Alaska Native" that are found in federal laws used to determine eligibility for federal programs and services specified in the law. It is not possible to present all Alaska Native definitions here but examples from different federal departments are provided below. Some of the other federal definitions include 1/4 blood quantum as criteria.

Bureau of Indian Affairs in Alaska

The Bureau of Indian Affairs provides a wide variety of services to enrolled Alaska Natives. BIA enrollment requires submission of an application for determination of the CDIB. Applicants must show relationship to an enrolled member(s) of a federally recognized Indian tribe, whether it is through birth mother or birth father, or both. A federally recognized Indian tribe means an Indian or Alaska Native tribe, band, nation, pueblo, village, or community which appears on the list of recognized tribes published in the Federal Register by the Secretary of the Interior (25 U.S.C. § 479a-1(a)). The degree of Indian blood is computed from lineal ancestors with Indian blood who were enrolled with a federally recognized Indian tribe or whose names appear on the designated base rolls of a federally recognized Indian tribe. The CDIB determination can be reported as a whole number (1), a fraction (3/4) or a decimal (.50) and will appear on the card issued by the BIA. **Alaska Natives enrolling through the Alaska BIA will have a CDIB determination based solely on the Alaska Native portion of their ancestry which will appear on their identification cards. However, tribal membership may or may not be included.** Native American ancestry from non-Alaska Natives is not shown on the BIA CDIB.

All Alaska Natives who receive a CDIB demonstrating their Alaska Native biological ancestry are eligible for BIA services. According to a BIA enrollment official who has been engaged in enrollment for over 10 years, individuals of "less than 1/64" Alaska Native blood quantum have been enrolled. It was recalled by the enrollment official that the person enrolled was descended from an Alaska Native born in 1909 that was 1/4 blood quantum. It was further stipulated that the enrolled person was eligible for all BIA services. Data presented elsewhere in this report show that three individuals of 1/128 Alaska Native ancestry have been enrolled since 2006.

Bureau of Indian Affairs Hiring Preference

The BIA has a hiring and promotion preference for Alaska Natives and American Indians. The following information was extracted from the BIA application for hire. Category A is for applicants who are members of federally-recognized Indian tribes, bands, or communities. For Category A, the application requires full name, enrollment number, date of birth, and tribal affiliation. The application is sent to the named tribe for verification of the enrollment claim based on "official tribal rolls…maintained by the BIA at the request of the tribe." There is no blood quantum requirement for the BIA Indian hiring preference if one is a member of a federally-recognized tribe. Categories B and C of the application for "Indians" who are not members of federally-recognized tribes are more restrictive. If the applicant is not a member of a federally-recognized tribe, then they must have 50% blood quantum.

Indian Health Service

Indian Health Service (IHS) programs are an entitlement the federal government is required to provide to Native Americans ("Indians") and Alaska Natives. Services are provided to persons who are of Indian and/or Alaska Native descent as evidenced by one or more of the following factors as listed in the Indian Health Manual 2-1.2 (Samuels 2014:147):

1. Is regarded by the community in which he lives as an Indian OR Alaska Native;
2. Is a member, enrolled or otherwise, of an Indian or Alaska Native Tribe or Group under Federal supervision;
3. Resides on tax-exempt land or owns restricted property;
4. Actively participates in tribal affairs;

Any other reasonable factor indicative of Indian descent.

In Alaska, IHS services are provided to Alaska Natives through the Alaska Native Medical Center and Alaska Native Regional Health Corporations, e.g., Yukon-Kuskokwim Health Corporation and Southeast Alaska Regional Health Consortium (SEARHC). The Alaska Native Health Center in Anchorage administers direct health services to individuals who meet one of the following descriptions:

- An Alaska Native person listed on the original Alaska Native Claims Settlement Act (ANCSA) roll;
- A lineal descendant of a person listed on the original ANCSA roll;
- A person holding a Certificate of Indian Blood (CIB) issued by the Bureau of Indian Affairs (BIA) or a federally recognized tribe;
- A person recognized as an official member of a federally recognized Indian tribe (excluding honorary or other non-constitutional or non-customary forms of membership).

Children of an eligible Alaska Native or American Indian, including:

- Non-Indian foster children;
- Adopted children;

- Stepchildren;
- Legal wards or orphans, until they reach the age of 19.

No blood quantum is used in any of the criteria for IHS eligibility in Alaska.

Yukon-Kuskokwim Health Corporation

In August, 2015, the Yukon-Kuskokwim Health Corporation (YKHC) issued the following statement:

> Attention IHS Beneficiaries: Starting August 1, 2015, patients who do not have a Certificate of Indian Blood (CIB) or Tribal enrollment information on file with YKHC may start receiving bills and be charged for medical services they receive at YKHC. If you receive a letter from YKHC saying we don't have your information, please bring a copy of your Tribal enrollment or CIB to the hospital, subregional clinic or village clinic at your next visit. YKHC is working with the Indian Health Service to keep records of AI/AN descendant beneficiaries, allowing us to sustain our funding and grow our health services in the future.

There are no further requirements for blood quantum – CIB card is sufficient to receive services.

Affordable Care Act

The Affordable Care Act (ACA), passed in 2009, provided new opportunities for health care coverage to Americans, especially those without health care insurance. A provision of the ACA known as the "individual mandate" requires that most Americans have health care coverage. If you don't have health care coverage for you and your family, you could be assessed a tax penalty. Alaska Native and American Indian people are exempt from this requirement, but, they must apply for this exemption. The original definition of Alaska Native promulgated by act administrators stipulated that only members of federally recognized tribes and shareholders of ANCSA corporations had the option to apply for the exemption when filing their taxes. Thousands of Alaska Natives would have missed out on benefits under the Affordable Care Act if the definition of Alaska Native under the law was not changed. The director of the Alaska Native Tribal Health Consortium estimated in October 2013 that the law's initial definition excluded about 14,000 Alaska Natives because of the requirement to be enrolled in a tribe or belong to a Native corporation.

Subsequently through lobbying efforts with the ACA administrators, assisted by staff of the Alaska delegation, an "administrative ruling" was promulgated in October 2014 that descendants, people with a Certificate Degree of Indian Blood (CDIB), and/or those eligible to receive services through a tribal health care provider would be able to claim the exemption when filing their taxes.

Indian Health Service Scholarship Program

This program has two different scholarships which do not have the same eligibility requirements. Tribal/Village membership eligibility requirements for each scholarship differ:

- Preparatory and Pre-Graduate Scholarships: Recipients must be a member or descendant of a federally recognized, state-recognized or terminated American Indian Tribe or Alaska Native village.
- Health Professions Scholarship: Recipients must be a member of a federally recognized American Indian Tribe or Alaska Native village only.

No blood quantum criteria are included in these eligibility requirements. This is an older definition for a program that does not recognize either ANCSA corporation membership, Alaska Native tribes per se, or CDIB as a means of establishing eligibility.

Indian Self-Determination and Education Assistance Act

The term "Indian tribe," at Section 4(e) of the Indian Self-Determination and Education Assistance Act, 25 U.S.C. § 450b(e) is defined as:

> "Indian tribe" means any Indian tribe, band, nation, or other organized group or community, including any Alaska Native village or regional or village corporation as defined in or established pursuant to the Alaska Native Claims Settlement Act (85 Stat. 688) [43 U.S.C. 1601 et seq.], which is recognized as eligible for the special programs and services provided by the United States to Indians because of their status as Indians...

Alaska Native organizations are included and equated with Indian tribes. There is no definition in the act of what constitutes "Indian" other than tribal membership.

Federal Regulations for the Bureau of Indian Affairs

"Alaska native" is defined in the Code of Federal Regulations in Title 25, Chapter I, Subchapter E, Part 36, as follows:

> (g) *Indian* means any person of Indian or Alaska native descent who is an enrolled member of any of those tribes listed or eligible to be listed in the FEDERAL REGISTER pursuant to 25 CFR 83.6 as recognized by and receiving services from the Bureau of Indian Affairs or a descendant of one-fourth degree or more Indian blood of an enrolled member; and any person not a member of one of the listed or eligible to be listed tribes who possesses at least one-half degree of Indian blood which is not derived from a tribe whose relationship is terminated by an Act of Congress.

In this three-part definition of "Indian," members of federally-recognized tribes receiving BIA services are deemed Indians but descendants of enrolled members must have 1/4 blood quantum. An indigenous claimant who is not a member of a federally-recognized tribe must demonstrate 1/2 degree of Indian blood.

Elsewhere in the same title for purposes of education, an "Indian student" is defined as "a student who is a member of an *Indian tribe* and is one-quarter (1/4) or more degree of *Indian* blood quantum."

US Department of Housing and Urban Development, Indian Home Loan Program

Section 184 of the Indian Home Loan program establishes a mortgage product specifically for American Indian and Alaska Native families, tribes, Alaska villages or tribally designated housing entities. Congress established this program in 1992 to facilitate homeownership in Native American communities. Eligible borrowers in Alaska for the Section 184 Indian Home Loan Program are 1) federally recognized tribes, 2) Alaska Native corporations formed pursuant to ANCSA, and 3) their members or shareholders. To establish eligibility for Section 184, applicants must provide documentation to verify their membership in a federally recognized tribe or ANCSA corporation. ANCSA corporations have enrolled members subject to the legislation and its amendments, and Alaska Native tribes establish their own rules for membership, maintain their own membership rolls, and house documentation of membership information for each enrollee. Therefore, the source of membership documentation is enrollment in a federally-recognized tribe or ANCSA corporation. BIA enrollment is not an option for eligibility. Blood or race is not the basis for eligibility, rather, organizational membership is. Accordingly, being a descendant of a member is not sufficient to be eligible for Section 184. The CDIB typically does not identify the tribal membership of the individual and is insufficient to document eligibility for the Section 184 program.

National Park Service

Federal laws and regulations may have specific purposes for defining Alaska Natives and American Indians. The National Park Service (NPS) recently listed a final rule entitled "Gathering of Certain Plants or Plant Parts by Federally Recognized Indian Tribes for Traditional Purposes" (Federal Register / Vol. 81, No. 133 / Doc. 2016-16434 / Tuesday, July 12, 2016). The rule authorizes the NPS to enter into agreements with federally recognized Indian tribes to allow for the gathering and removal of plants or plant parts from National Park Service system areas for traditional purposes. It further specifies that, "Only enrolled members of a federally recognized tribe will be allowed to collect plants or plant parts, and the tribe must be traditionally associated with the specific park area." The plant gathering must meet a traditional purpose that is a customary activity and practice rooted in the history of the tribe and is important for the continuation of the tribe's distinct culture. The definition in this rule authorizes Indians who are "enrolled members of a federally recognized tribe" to engage in the designated activities.

Alaska Native Regional Corporations

While the definition of "Alaska Native" under federal law and federal agency regulations is crucial for the provision of federal services to Alaska Natives, Alaska Natives themselves have addressed the definition for their own organization, Alaska Native corporations, under constraints of the original ANCSA legislation and subsequent amendments. In ANCSA, Alaska Natives who were 1/4 degree or more Alaska Indian, Eskimo, or Aleut blood, or a combination were eligible to enroll. In 1988, Congress amended ANCSA to allow corporations to issue new stock to those born after the original date for eligibility, which was December 18, 1971. Original membership criteria for ANCSA enrollment was specified in Section 3 and provisions for enrollment in Section 5. The new amendment in

1988 to Section 7 provided for corporations to enroll additional stockholders, including Alaska Natives born after 1971. A number of options for new stock were recognized. New recipients might receive stock equivalent to that of original shareholders or stock with limitations on transmissibility, voting rights, and receipt of dividends.

Since 1988, a number of Alaska Native regional and village corporations have provided for issuing to Alaska Natives born post-1971. The table below summarizes the provisions that have been adopted by six regional corporations. With the exception of Calista, the corporations utilize 1/4 blood quantum for issuance of new stock. Other than Calista, such stock is lifetime stock that disappears on the death of the holder—it cannot be transferred or inherited.

Some village and merged village corporations have also created programs for enrolling new shareholders. Their criteria for enrollment and the kinds of stock that new enrollees receive vary considerably.

Table 3 Alaska Native Regional Corporation policies for accepting new shareholders	
Ahtna	Applicants must be a lineal descendant of an original Ahtna shareholder and have 1/4 or more Alaska Native blood quantum.
Arctic Slope	Applicants must be a first or second generation descendant of original shareholder. Two classes of new stock are recognized: Class C is equivalent common stock requiring 1/4 blood quantum as originally stipulated in ANCSA and Class D is other stock intended for descendants of original shareholders (who have less than 1/4 Alaska Native blood quantum but greater than zero blood quantum).
Calista	Applicants must be a descendant of an original shareholder – no blood quantum is required. New issues hold same amount of class C stock as that given to original issuees and the new stock provides for both voting rights and dividends.
Doyon	Applicants must be a child of an original Doyon shareholder and of 1/4 or more Alaska Native blood quantum.
NANA	Applicants must be descendant of original shareholder and of 1/4 blood quantum.
Sealaska	Applicants must be descendant of original shareholder and of 1/4 blood quantum.

Summation

Definitions currently used by the Alaska BIA and IHS for determining Alaska Native eligibility for the provision of services do not include a blood quantum level but require some form of proof, such as the CDIB, of Alaska Native ancestry. In addition, non-Native women married to Native men who are pregnant with the husband's child are also eligible for IHS services. There are other federal definitions of "Indian" or "Alaska Native" that do use 1/4 blood quantum. There are numerous definitions of Alaska Natives in federal laws that have specific purposes and use different criteria. Blood quantum of 1/4 and descent from an original shareholder has been used in criteria for the issuance of new stock under 1988 amendments to ANCSA by five of six Alaska Native regional corporations from whom information was obtained. Calista alone requires lineal descent from an original shareholder for enrollment of new shareholders but has no blood quantum requirement.

BLOOD QUANTUM ELIGIBILITY TRENDS

Study Objective 3. Determine if a standard of 1/4 blood quantum for activities covered by the MMPA is or could result in eligibility issues for certain Alaska Native populations.

Trends in regard to the blood quantum characteristics of Alaska Natives are discussed in this section with special attention paid to the topic of the proportion of various populations falling below the 1/4 blood quantum MMPA regulatory requirement. The topic of blood quantum in general is extremely sensitive and controversial among Alaska Natives as was repeatedly evident during the course of this research. Three lines of evidence are covered in the following discussion—qualitative data based on interviews and comments, numerical data from various sources, and regional hub tribal perspectives obtained through interviews with tribal leaders. Hard data on numbers of Alaska Natives of less than 1/4 blood quantum and the frequency of their membership in various Alaska Native organizations are difficult to obtain for various reasons. Tribes vary substantially in their requirements for enrollment – some utilize the 1/4 blood quantum, some use only lineal descent from original enrollees, some accept Native Americans who are not Alaska Natives, and some have individual requirements. Few have the data readily available even if 1/4 blood quantum is used as a criterion. ANCSA corporations that are engaged in the process of shareholder enrollment likely have data on the blood quantum characteristics of new shareholder applicants but it is proprietary and would probably not be generally available. The BIA enrollment office does have data on blood quantum of enrolled Alaska Natives in their records and data on blood quantum of new CDIB recipients between July 2006 and July 2016 have been provided for this report. The data are discussed in the next section.

Qualitative Data

Qualitative data consists of commentary by a variety of persons in meetings, in personal discussions, and on other occasions about the MMPA regulatory definition and how it relates to their personal, familial experiences, or others of which they are aware.

The significance of marine mammal harvests for food and materials to be available to current descendants who are not eligible under the MMPA regulatory definition as well as for future generations was a recurrent topic, especially in the southern Alaska Native region. In some cases, commentators expressed very strong views about their intent and right to pass on cultural traditions of marine mammal use to their descendants even if they were not eligible under the regulations. Community leaders in all regions are concerned that the blood quantum limit, if used to exclude young people with less than 1/4 blood quantum from learning their parents' traditions, will be a self-fulfilling prophecy, in that it will prevent a portion of a generation from becoming full members of the community. They fear, not unreasonably, that this will eventually lead to larger cultural death and is thus an existential threat to their persistence as a distinctive people. The topic was also addressed, but less frequently, by Alaska Natives from western and northern Alaska.

On several occasions, older women expressed their deep pain in not being able to pass on their handicraft traditions to grandchildren of less than 1/4 blood quantum. This was especially troubling when the young girls expressed an interest in learning when they saw them working on the handicrafts.

Voorhees (2015), in her work with the Nanuuq Commission, noted that "again and again [she] heard hunters voice fear and awareness of the 1/4 blood quantum limit that could conceivably exclude their descendants" from utilization of marine mammals. Similarly, on several occasions older men noted that they were deeply troubled by the fact that some of their male grandchildren were eligible so they were taken out hunting but other male grandchildren were not eligible and so they were not taken. Grandchildren who could not participate were confused and hurt by their inability to do things that they perceived were of great significance to their parents and grandparents.

Alaska Native co-management institutions pro-actively seek to sustain the use of marine mammals and the cultural, nutritional, and other values associated with their use. It is clearly recognized by co-management board members for species utilized in the southern, Gulf of Alaska region that the continuity of those traditions depends on insuring that communities have hunters who will be able to harvest the animals. The following are examples of those activities.

One of the goals of the Alaska Native Harbor Seal Commission (ANHSC) is to increase the use of harbor seal as food. The medicinal values of seal oil and its important use in preservation and preparation of other foods are well recognized. The commission has prepared brochures and handouts on how to prepare oil and other foods which were handed out to board members for distribution at the spring 2016 meeting. In addition, the materials are also available on the commission's website.

At their spring 2016 meeting, the Alaska Sea Otter and Sea Lion Commission conducted an all day workshop on marine mammal hunting, processing, and utilization. In addition, traditional ecological knowledge and appropriate ritual behavior toward the marine mammals was taught. Young hunters, primarily from Kodiak villages, were brought to the workshop for training.

Numerical Data

Numerical data were acquired during the research to examine the current status of Alaska Natives in regard to blood quantum percentage distribution. These data include 1) projections of the blood quantum proportions of original Sealaska shareholders over two generations of descendants by 2008, 2) information from Sealaska on blood quantum of recent applicants for scholarships who are either enrolled or descendants, 3) information from the Sitka Tribe of Alaska on membership and blood quantum characteristics, 4) BIA enrollment information showing number of enrollees from 2006-2016 with CDIB less than 25% blood quantum by blood quantum percentage, and 5) BIA enrollment information on all CDIBs issued from 7/2006 to 7/2016 organized by region where determinable. The data show the number enrolled by percentages below 1/4 as well as the number of blood quantum enrollees of less than 25% by region from 2006 to 2016.

Sealaska Corporation Data. In consideration of the future of Sealaska Corporation and the issuance of stock to shareholders born after the enactment of ANCSA, the shareholder committee of Sealaska commissioned two studies on the demographic future of the corporation. The question of "dilution" and potential impact on corporate functioning was a significant consideration in the decision to examine the data. The initial study was completed in 2002 and a second was completed in 2005 updating the data and projections of the earlier study. Table 4 presents hard data on the blood quantum of the original group of Sealaska shareholders and their descendants (children and grandchildren) born between 1974-2001.

Two points of significance in regards to the topic of interest need to be highlighted. First, the proportion of the descendant population of less than 25% blood quantum, and therefore ineligible under the MMPA criteria for Alaska Native, had reached 30% by 2001. Second, despite the increase in the ineligible portion of the population, the cohort of the population over 25% had increased the total overall population of eligible MMPA hunters by 13,677 which exceeded the initial shareholder cohort of 13,722 (Table 4). Assuming that roughly 10,000 original shareholders were still living, this would mean that the total Sealaska original and descendant population eligible under the MMPA had more than doubled.

This information tells us nothing about the actual number of Sealaska shareholders and descendants who participated in MMPA authorized activities with marine mammals.

Table 4 Blood quantum of original Sealaska population in 1973 and descendants of shareholders and children born from 1974-2001

Original shareholders and descendants	Total	100%	75-99%	50-74%	25-49%	<25%
Births to shareholders and descendants	19,484	1,126	1,334	4,335	6,882	5,807
Percentage of total		5.80%	6.80%	22.20%	35.30%	29.80%
Original shareholders	13,722	3,843	1,619	4,169	3,973	na
Percentage of total		28.00%	11.80%	30.40%	29%	na

Source: Passel 2002, Table 4

Table 5 presents data taken from the 2005 study that makes projections about blood quantum proportion of cohorts through 2011. The numbers are based on assumptions from the previous hard data on actual blood quantum proportions of descendants through 2001. Data from this study project that by 2004, there were 21,468 descendants of which slightly fewer than half, 9,910 (46%), would be less than 1/4 blood quantum (Edmonston 2005: 7). The study further projects that by 2008 there would be 32,424 descendants of whom 19,157 or 59% will be less than 1/4 blood quantum. Assuming 10,181 original shareholders still living, over 19,000 of new Sealaska shareholders or 59% would be ineligible to utilize marine mammals under the current regulatory definition. These figures are projections made nearly a decade ago. When they are compared to CDIB enrollment data from 2011-2016 presented below, the projections appear to overstate the increase in number of Sealaska descendants with less than 1/4 blood quantum that was expected.

Table 5 Original Sealaska shareholders and lineal descendants, by blood quantum, at end of year for 1973, 2004, and 2008

Shareholders and descendants	Original shareholders	Total shareholders	1/4+	1/8 to 1/4	Less than 1/8
1973 original shareholders	13,722	13,722	13,604	dkn	dkn
Percentage of total			99.1%	N/A	N/A
2004 shareholder and descendant projections	10,792	21,468	11,558	6,664	3,246
Percentage of total			53.80%	31.00%	15.10%
2008 shareholder and descendant projections	10,181	32,424	13,267	13,111	6,046
Percentage of total			40.90%	40.40%	18.60%

Source: Edmonston 2005, Table 1

Table 6 presents data provided by Sealaska Corporation on blood quantum levels of applicants for scholarships in 2014-2015 and 2015-2016. While ages of applicants are not included, the age of the college cohort probably falls between 18 and 30 years of age with possibly a few slightly older. Approximately 40% of these scholarship applicants do not reside in Alaska. In 2014-2015, 40.4% of 539 applicants were less than 1/4 blood quantum and in 2015-2016, 39.4% of 426 applicants were less than 1/4 blood quantum. In both years, this group (those with less than 1/4 blood quantum) comprised the most numerous cohort of applicants by quartile. Thus the most numerous quartile of Sealaska scholarship applicants in the last two years would be ineligible to either hunt marine mammals or to manufacture handicrafts from marine mammal materials as a result of being less than 1/4 blood quantum.

The proportion of Sealaska scholarship applicants for 2014-2015 and 2015-2016 that are below 1/4 blood quantum is about 40%, which is comparable to the proportion of CDIB enrollees from the Sealaska region for 2011-2016 who are less than 1/4 blood quantum, at 42.8% (see Table 12). These data contrast with the projections data presented in Table 5.

Table 6 Sealaska data on recent scholarship applicants

Blood quantum	Students (out of 539)	Percentage of students
	2014–2015	
Under 25%	218 students	40.40%
25-49%	214 students	40.00%
50-74%	80 students	14.80%
75-99%	17 students	3.15%
100%	10 students	1.85%
	2015–2016	
Under 25%	168 students	39.40%
25-49%	167 students	39.20%
50-74%	65 students	15.25%
75-99%	19 students	4.46%
100%	7 students	1.64%

Source: Sealaska Heritage Institute

Sitka Tribe of Alaska. According to Mike Miller, Chair of IPCoMM and the Sitka Marine Mammal Commission, Sitka Tribe of Alaska has over 5,100 members about 50% of whom are 1/4 or more blood quantum. He also reported that some Sitka Tribe of Alaska members are Native Americans (American Indians) who transferred their membership from tribes in the continental United States.

BIA CDIB Enrollment Data. Data provided by the BIA enrollment office concerning CDIB enrollments between July 1, 2006 and July 8, 2016 are discussed in this section. Data was provided on the number of Alaska Natives enrolled of less than 1/4 blood quantum by percentage and fraction (for example 1/8, 1/16 etc.). Data was provided on Alaska Native CDIB enrollees by regional affiliation over the same period showing total enrollees and the number of enrollees with less than 1/4 blood quantum. For the data on those of less than 1/4 blood quantum by percentage only cumulative data are presented. For the data on regional affiliation, cumulative data for 2006-2016 is presented as well as data for the periods 2006-2011 and 2011-2016.

CDIB enrollees of less than 1/4 blood quantum by percent of blood quantum. Figure 1 displays the number of Alaska Natives enrolled between July 1, 2006 and July 8, 2016 of less than 25% by blood quantum percentage. Actual data provided by the BIA enrollment office recorded the number of individuals of each blood quantum by percentage and fraction. The data have been grouped into the five ranges under 25% that are displayed. Nearly 20,000 Alaska Natives of less than 25% blood quantum were enrolled during the period. Eight persons were enrolled with 1/128 blood quantum, the lowest of any enrollee recorded.

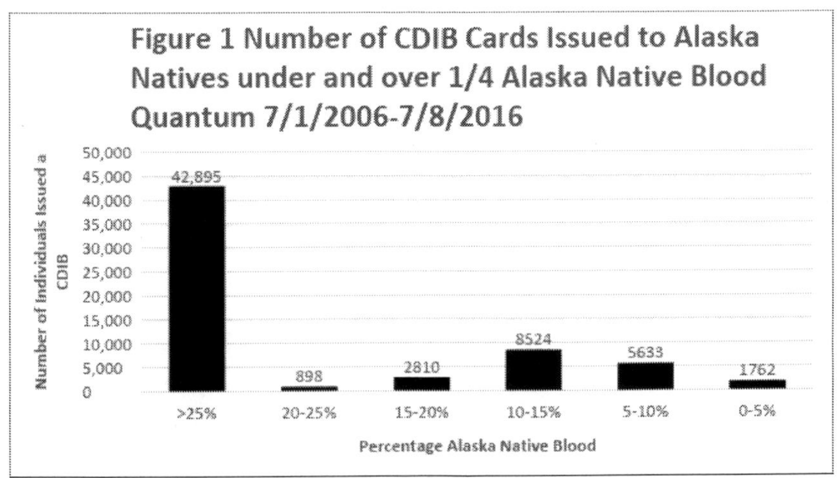

CDIB enrollees by regional affiliation. Table 7 shows data on all Alaska Native CDIB enrollees and those with less than 1/4 blood quantum by regional affiliation from July 1, 2006-July 8, 2016. During the designated period, a total of 62,522 persons were issued new CDIBs of which 31.03% were less than 1/4 Alaska Native blood quantum. A portion of the enrollees, 11,642 (18.6%), could not be assigned to a regional affiliation due primarily to the fact that they were descendants with parentage from more than one regional group. As descendants, 36.2% of the unassigned cohort were less than 1/4 blood quantum, a rate 20% higher than the regionally affiliated cohorts.

The two Alaska Native regions with the highest number of enrollees under 1/4 blood quantum were Sealaska, 11,529 (18.4%), and Calista, 9,234 (14.8). No other region exceeded 5,500 enrollees.

Table 7 CDIBs issued to Alaska Natives less than 1/4 Alaska Native blood quantum from 7/1/2006-7/8/2016

Alaska regional affiliation	Number issued (less than one-fourth)	All entries for region in same timeframe	% of CDIB enrollees w/ less than one-fourth
No values in database	4216	11642	36.20%
Ahtna	230	880	26.10%
Aleut	690	1857	37.20%
Arctic Slope	228	1556	14.70%
Bering Straits	741	4017	18.40%
Bristol Bay	1116	3415	32.70%
Calista	689	9234	7.50%
Chugach	893	1578	56.60%
Cook Inlet	3036	5117	59.30%
Doyon	1478	5190	28.50%
Koniag	1485	2517	59.00%
NANA	344	2635	13.10%
Sealaska	3684	11529	32.00%
The 13th Region	797	1355	58.80%
TOTAL RECORDS	19627	62522	31.03%

The next two tables divide the cumulative data from 2006-2016 into two periods. Table 8 displays data for the period July 1, 2006-July 8, 2011. During the designated period, a total of 34,597 persons were issued new CDIBs of which 28.2% were less than 1/4 Alaska Native blood quantum. A portion of the enrollees, 991 (2.9%), could not be assigned to a regional affiliation due primarily to the fact that they were descendants with parentage from more than one regional group. As descendants, 33.8% of the unassigned cohort were less than 1/4 blood quantum, a rate 20% higher than the regionally affiliated cohorts.

The two Alaska Native regions with the highest number of enrollees were Sealaska, 6,943 (20.0% of enrollees), and Calista, 6,376 (18.4% of enrollees). The two regions differed significantly in the proportion of enrollees under 1/4 blood quantum. For Sealaska, 24.8% of new CDIB enrollees were under 1/4 blood quantum while for Calista, the comparable figure was 7.0%. No other region exceeded 4,000 enrollees.

Table 8 CDIBs issued to Alaska Natives less than 1/4 Alaska Native blood quantum from 7/1/2006-7/8/2011

Alaska regional affiliation	Number issued (less than one-fourth)	All entries for region in same timeframe	% of CDIB enrollees w/ less than one-fourth
No Values in Database	335	991	33.80%
Ahtna	146	678	21.50%
Aleut	481	1389	34.60%
Arctic Slope	153	993	15.40%
Bering Straits	431	2531	17.00%
Bristol Bay	706	2392	29.50%
Calista	446	6376	7.00%
Chugach	651	1185	54.90%
Cook Inlet	2223	3789	58.70%
Doyon	794	3164	25.10%
Koniag	1010	1830	55.20%
NANA	197	1535	12.80%
Sealaska	1720	6943	24.80%
The 13th Region	487	801	60.80%
TOTAL RECORDS	**9780**	**34597**	**28.20%**

Table 9 CDIBs Issued to Alaska Natives less than 1/4 Alaska Native blood quantum from 7/1/2011-7/8/2016			
Alaska regional affiliation	Number issued (less than one-fourth)	All entries for region in same timeframe	% of CDIB enrollees w/ less than one-fourth
No values in database	3881	10651	36.40%
Ahtna	84	202	41.60%
Aleut	209	468	44.70%
Arctic Slope	75	563	13.30%
Bering Straits	310	1486	20.90%
Bristol Bay	410	1023	40.10%
Calista	243	2858	8.50%
Chugach	242	393	61.60%
Cook Inlet	813	1328	61.20%
Doyon	684	2026	33.80%
Koniag	475	687	69.10%
NANA	147	1100	13.40%
Sealaska	1964	4586	42.80%
The 13th Region	310	554	56.00%
TOTAL RECORDS	**9847**	**27925**	**35.20%**

Table 9 displays data for the period July 1, 2011-July 8, 2016. During the designated period, a total of 27,925 persons were issued new CDIBs of which 35.2% were less than 1/4 Alaska Native blood quantum. A portion of the enrollees, 10,651 (38.1%), could not be assigned to a regional affiliation due primarily to the fact that they were descendants with parentage from more than one regional group. If accurate, this number of unassigned Alaska Natives represents a massive increase in the number from the previous time period. As descendants, 36.4% of the unassigned cohort were less than 1/4 blood quantum, a rate slightly higher than the regionally affiliated cohorts but close to the rate for the previous period as reported in Table 8.

The two Alaska Native regions with the highest number of enrollees were Sealaska, 4,586 (16.4 of enrollees), and Calista, 2,858 (10.2% of enrollees), although their proportion of total Alaska Native enrollments declined substantially from the previous period. The two regions differed significantly in the proportion of enrollees under 1/4 blood quantum. For Sealaska, 42.8% of new CDIB enrollees were under 1/4 blood quantum, a 75% increase from the previous period. While for Calista, the comparable figure was 8.5%, also an increase but only about 20%. No other region exceeded 2,100 enrollees.

The next three tables display the same data but for only the coastal regions where Alaska Natives are eligible to harvest marine mammals. Table 10 reports data for the entire period from 2006-2016. For all coastal Natives, the rate of newly enrolled CDIBs under 1/4 blood quantum is 29.7% over this period. This rate is slightly lower than that for all Alaska Natives, 28.2% over the same period. The difference appears because the unassigned are not included in the coastal cohort. However, it should be noted that some of the unassigned no doubt belong to the coastal Natives cohort.

The data indicate that the coastal Alaska Native regions fall roughly into three groups based on CDIB enrollment blood quantum percentages. Four groups in western Alaska have rates of new CDIBs under 1/4 blood quantum of 20% or less. These are, from lowest to highest, Calista, NANA, Arctic Slope, and Bering Straits. The second group of three regional groups displays intermediate rates of CDIB enrollment below 1/4 blood quantum between 32% and 38%. These are, from lowest to highest, Sealaska, Bristol Bay, and Aleut. The third group with the highest percentage enrollees of under 1/4 blood quantum ranges from 56% to 59%. From lowest to highest the groups are Chugach, Koniag, and Cook Inlet.

What accounts for the differences between the regions? Two reasons appear most likely. The first reason is the history of contact in different parts of Alaska. Regions along the Gulf of Alaska came into direct contact with outsiders much earlier and have been in contact much longer. Some outsiders from the earliest periods settled in the region. One result was intermarriage between the groups which continued over the decades since the late 1700s, especially in the central and western Gulf of Alaska regions. Another wave of outsiders coming to the southern regions was brought by the onset of the commercial canned salmon industry in the 1880s that also resulted in a substantial amount of intermixing. This means that the southern groups had many more individuals of mixed blood quantum than elsewhere in Alaska. By contrast, groups from western Bristol Bay to the Arctic Slope encountered outsiders much later and few remained in the region thus reducing rates of admixture. Communities of the Calista region are most extreme in this regard with many of them not encountering sustained interaction with outsiders until the first decades of the 20th century. The second reason for the differences has to do with presence of large concentrations of non-Natives in proximity to Native regional groups. In this regard, clearly Cook Inlet but also Chugach and Koniag regional groups are in close and more frequent contact with non-Natives than western and northern Alaska Natives.

Table 10 CDIBs issued to coastal Alaska Natives less than 1/4 Alaska Native blood quantum from 7/01/2006-7/08/2016

Alaska regional affiliation	Number issued (less than one-fourth)	All entries for region in same timeframe	% of CDIB enrollees with less than one-fourth
Calista	689	9234	7.50%
NANA	344	2635	13.10%
Arctic Slope	228	1556	14.60%
Bering Straits	741	4017	18.40%
Sealaska	3684	11529	32.00%
Bristol Bay	1116	3415	32.70%
Aleut	690	1857	37.10%
Chugach	893	1578	56.60%
Koniag	1485	2517	59.00%
Cook Inlet	3036	5117	59.30%
TOTAL RECORDS	12906	43455	29.70%

Tables 11 and 12 provide data on two sub-periods from 2006-2011 and from 2011-2016. It is noteworthy than the total number of CDIBs issued for the coastal Alaska Native regional groups dropped by approximately 1/3 over this period. Two possible reasons for the steep decline are 1) the increase in the number of unassigned individuals receiving CDIBs who are descendants whose ancestry comes from several regional groups and 2) decline in birth rates.

Table 11 CDIBs issued to coastal Alaska Natives less than 1/4 Alaska Native blood quantum from 7/2006-7/2011

Alaska regional affiliation	Number issued (less than one-fourth)	All entries for region in same timeframe	% of CDIB enrollees with less than one-fourth
Calista	446	6376	7.00%
NANA	197	1535	12.80%
Arctic Slope	153	993	15.40%
Bering Straits	431	2531	17.00%
Sealaska	1720	6943	24.80%
Bristol Bay	706	2392	29.50%
Aleut	481	1389	34.60%
Chugach	651	1185	54.90%
Koniag	1010	1830	55.20%
Cook Inlet	2223	3789	58.70%
Total Records	**8018**	**28963**	**27.70%**

Several important points emerge from comparing the data on CDIB enrollments for coastal Natives during the two periods.

The percentage of CDIB enrollees under 1/4 blood quantum increased from 27.7% to 33.7%, which at 22%, is a very substantial increase. In keeping with the overall percentage increase in under 1/4 blood quantum CDIB enrollees, all but one of the regional groups showed an increase in the percentage of enrollees under 1/4 blood quantum. The exception is the Arctic Slope region, which declined from a rate of 15.4% to 13.3%, a 15.8% drop.

Table 12 CDIBs issued to coastal Alaska Natives less than 1/4 Alaska Native blood quantum from 7/1/2011-7/8/2016			
Alaska regional affiliation	Number issued (less than one-fourth)	All entries for region in same timeframe	% of CDIB enrollees with less than one-fourth
Calista	243	2858	8.50%
NANA	147	1100	13.40%
Arctic Slope	75	563	13.30%
Bering Straits	310	1486	20.90%
Bristol Bay	410	1023	40.10%
Sealaska	1964	4586	42.80%
Aleut	209	468	44.70%
Chugach	242	393	61.60%
Koniag	475	687	69.10%
Cook Inlet	813	1328	61.20%
TOTAL RECORDS	**4888**	**14492**	**33.70%**

Table 13 identifies the rates of CDIB enrollment increase or decrease for the nine coastal regions between 2006-2011 and 2011-2016. The rates of percentage increase for the nine groups again fall into three groupings: low, intermediate, and high. Four of the regional groups show low rates of percentage increase at +2.5% or less. These are:

- Nana 0.3%
- Calista 1.5%
- Cook Inlet 1.9%
- Bering Straits 2.5%

Two of the regional groups show intermediate rates of percentage increase between 5% and 7.5%. These are:

- Chugach 5.0%
- Aleut 7.5%

Three of the regional groups show high rates of percentage increase of 10% of above. These are:

- Koniag 10.1%
- Bristol Bay 10.6%
- Sealaska 10.8%

Table 13 Changes in Percentage of 1/4 Blood Quantum Enrollees of Coastal Alaska Native Regional Groups Between 2006-2011 and 2011-2016

Coastal Alaska Native Regional Groups	Percent Increase or Decrease	
Arctic Slope	-	2.10%
Nana	+	0.30%
Calista	+	1.50%
Cook Inlet	+	1.90%
Bering Straits	+	2.50%
Chugach	+	5.00%
Aleut	+	7.50%
Koniag	+	10.10%
Bristol Bay	+	10.60%
Sealaska	+	10.80%

Regional Hub Tribal Perspectives

During the research, many people at organizational presentations and in interviews mentioned that tribes were the preferred entities to decide who is eligible to participate in marine mammal hunting and handicraft manufacturing activities. As it was not feasible to contact and interact with all of Alaska Native coastal tribes to address the issue of the current impact of the 1/4 blood quantum on marine mammal hunting and handicraft manufacturing of tribal members and their descendants, a decision was made to contact the tribes in the regional hubs to obtain information as best as possible on the issue. The reasons for this decision are that 1) regional hubs have substantially greater populations than villages and 2) are more likely to have residents, tribal members, or descendants who are of less than 1/4 blood quantum and therefore ineligible to hunt or utilize marine mammals under the current regulation than the surrounding villages they serve.

The topics of interviews with regional hub tribal heads were 1) number of current enrolled members, 2) enrollment criteria—specifically did they use 1/4 blood quantum, 3) what number or proportion of the tribal enrollment was less than 1/4 (if they didn't use blood quantum as enrollment criteria, an estimate was requested), and 4) were they aware of families with children or grandchildren that were ineligible under the 1/4 blood quantum requirement of the MMPA.

Barrow (Native Village of Barrow) – 3,600 members. Organized under the IRA. No estimate concerning those of less than 1/4 blood quantum but there are some families with members who probably don't qualify. Lineal descendants of an original enrollee is the current criteria for membership. An issue mentioned was there are 300 local Natives who have CDIB and apparently believe they are enrolled but are in fact not on the tribal roles as they have not submitted applications for membership to the tribe.

Bethel (Orutsararmuit Native Council) – 3,100 members. Current enrollment criteria are 1/4 blood quantum and descendant from a Bethel tribal member. Unknown whether or not the 1/4 blood quantum is affecting eligibility to hunt or utilize marine mammals.

Cordova (Eyak Tribe) – 420 active members. As of 2015, 56% of tribe was 1/4 or more. Enrollment of those demonstrating lineal descent from original enrollees without regard to blood quantum is the current practice. There are families and persons who are ineligible to hunt or use marine mammals under the MMPA regulatory criteria.

Dillingham (Curyung) – 2,800 members. Estimated that 60% are possibly 1/4 or more. The current criteria for membership is lineal descent from an original enrollee. The impact of the MMPA regulation on marine mammal hunting by tribal members is unknown.

Juneau (Douglas Indian Association) – 700 approximate members. The current criteria for tribal membership is 1/4 blood quantum, descendant from original enrollee or tribal member, and resident in community for one year. Commentators are aware of families who have descendants that are ineligible but if they are less than 1/4 blood quantum those members are not enrolled.

Kodiak (Sun'aq) – 1,738 members. Sun'aq became federally recognized in 2000. They did not appear on 1988 or 1993 lists published in the federal register. The tribe then reached out and worked through the Alaska Congressional delegation to be recognized. They received a letter from the BIA in 2000 stating they were a tribe. The current enrollment practice is descendant from a tribal member or original enrollee. It is estimated that over 50% of the tribal membership is less than 1/4 blood quantum.

Nome (Eskimo Community of Nome) – 2,900 members. IRA based tribe. Enroll lineal descendants but also have a substantial number of transfers from nearby tribes—Council, for example. It is unknown what number are under 1/4 blood quantum. It is likely that there are a number of families that have descendants who are not eligible. Some do hunt for their families even though they are less than 1/4 blood quantum.

Kotzebue (Native Village of Kotzebue) – 3,200 members. IRA based tribe. Enroll lineal descendants with no blood quantum. A rough estimate is that less than 20% of total enrollees are of less than 1/4 blood quantum. Tribal council members indicated that there may be individuals of less than 1/4 blood quantum hunting, but they did not know for sure.

Ketchikan (Ketchikan Indian Corporation) – 5,600 members. Lineal descendant is used for enrollment or transfer from another federally-recognized tribe. No estimate provided of enrollees with less than 1/4 blood quantum but it is thought to be substantial.

Sitka (Sitka Tribe of Alaska) – 5,100 members. Approximately 50% are less than 1/4 blood quantum. The Sitka Tribe has created a Marine Mammal Commission from which those members desiring to hunt marine mammals must obtain a permit to hunt in Sitka Tribe's traditional territory. Only applicants who meet the MMPA regulatory definition of 1/4 blood quantum or more are eligible to receive permits.

Summation

Both qualitative and numerical data demonstrate that the proportion of the Alaska Native population falling below the 1/4 blood quantum has been increasing for some time. CDIB enrollment data shows that groups vary substantially in regard to the number of new enrollees under 1/4 blood quantum. For several groups residing along the Gulf of Alaska, rates of CDIBs issued between 2011–2016 are above 50%. These data indicate that the proportion of the Alaska Native population becoming ineligible to hunt marine mammals under current agency enforcement policies is rising at an accelerating rate. The result may be that in some communities around the Gulf of Alaska there may be few individuals eligible to hunt or utilize marine mammals in the not too distant future.

ALTERNATIVE CRITERIA FOR DETERMINATION OF ALASKA NATIVE ELIGIBILITY

Study Objective 4. Identify and examine alternative criteria to 1/4 blood quantum that could be proposed including but not limited to 1/8 blood quantum, tribal membership, BIA enrollment, local/regional cultural determination, lineal descendant, or other criteria that might be identified during the research.

In this section, a number of alternative criteria for Alaska Native eligibility that have been identified during the course of the research are presented and discussed. The discussion will also briefly describe what would be needed in the law by amendment, by changing the regulatory definition, or by administrative action (if possible) of some kind.

Blood Quantum Changed to 1/8

Changing the eligibility requirement to 1/8 blood quantum would continue the use of blood quantum and meet some issues of eligibility for Alaska Natives currently ineligible. Alaska Native marine mammal hunters would have to be enrolled by BIA and have a CDIB of 1/8 or higher or be enrolled in a tribe that enrolls members of 1/8 blood quantum or greater. However, there is currently a substantial cohort of persons who are of less than 1/8 blood quantum (see discussion in objective 3). In addition, through time and intermarriage, lineally descended individuals would continue to be born who are less than 1/8 blood quantum and the same situation of ineligibility would arise for them. This change would allow for an expansion of eligibility less than using CDIB. The change to 1/8 would require an amendment to the law or a change in the regulatory definition.

Tribal Enrollment

Tribes as domestic dependent nations determine their own criteria for membership under current federal law. However, tribal membership criteria must be submitted to the BIA for review when changes are sought by the tribe. While a large number of Alaska Natives are enrolled in tribes, some are not, so those not enrolled would be ineligible if tribal enrollment were the sole criteria for MMPA determination.

Tribal enrollment criteria vary substantially across Alaska. Under the current MMPA regulatory definition, tribal members would more than likely have to be demonstrably of Alaska Native descent of 1/4 blood quantum as the regulations are presently interpreted unless the blood quantum requirement were eliminated. Many Alaska Native tribes allow the enrollment of Native Americans who are not Alaska Native through transfer if they can demonstrate tribal enrollment elsewhere and meet other criteria such as residency. Examples include Alaska Native spouses who are Native Americans. It is unlikely that such tribal members would be eligible under MMPA which in the law stipulates that the exemption is for Alaska Natives. Other Alaska Native tribes require residency of some period of time in order to be enrolled or considered an "active" tribal member. Tribal enrollment lists in such cases can include "active" and "inactive" members. Some tribes have a strict lineal descendant policy that accepts new members only if they can demonstrate one of the original tribal enrollees was an ancestor. The demonstration must be of direct descent. Some tribes combine lineal descent with blood quantum (typically 1/4) while others only use lineal descent and do not have a blood quantum requirement. At what age a person can enroll also varies among tribes. Some tribes allow enrollment as early as the age of 2 while others do not allow enrollment until 18. One problem that was identified in several discussions was the issue of double enrollment. Persons are allowed to be members of only one tribe at any time. Tribes indicated that in order for a member of another tribe to be enrolled, they would have to file and receive a "disenrollment" form from the other tribe.

There appear to be several ways by which tribal enrollment could be used for MMPA eligibility determination. It could be accomplished by amending the law and specifying tribal enrollment as the sole or one of several means of identifying an Alaska Native. It could be accomplished by changing the regulations and specifying tribal enrollment as the sole or one of several means of identifying an Alaska Native. It might possibly be accomplished by NMFS and USFWS either publishing a "policy statement," an "administrative ruling," or an "understanding" that would specify tribal enrollment as an acceptable means of a person being identified as an Alaska Native under the "regarded as" language in the regulatory definition of Alaska Native.

Tribal Enrollment and Certification

Carol Daniels (2011), former AFN attorney who did extensive research on the issue of MMPA Native eligibility criteria in 2010-2011, suggested that a two-tiered process of eligibility establishment consisting of tribal membership and certification could be an alternative way to determine eligibility under the MMPA. Her proposal was based on the Indian Arts and Crafts Act of 1990, 18 U.S.C. § 1159 (1994), 25 U.S.C. § 305 (1994), which provided for the certification of "Indian artist." Through the tribal certification procedure tribes would have final say regarding who is considered an

"Indian artist." The Act defines "Indian" as "any individual who is a member of an Indian tribe." However, the act also allows an Indian tribe to certify non-Indians as "Indian artists" if their art products are of the tribal style. In addition, as noted in the discussion of the ACA exemption above, there are a substantial number of Alaska Natives who are not members of tribes.

Nevertheless, a similar approach could be taken with respect to the definition of Alaska Native for purposes of the MMPA. "Alaska Native" could be defined as an individual who is a member of an Indian tribe, or certified as an Indian, Eskimo, or Aleut by an Indian tribe. Certification would be left up to tribes but would at a minimum indicate that the person was of Alaska Native ancestry. This would leave the decision as to who qualifies to the individual tribes who could use additional standards as discussed earlier in the section on tribes. For communities who believe that non-Natives living in or married into the community, the tribal certification approach may be a way to allow those individuals to become eligible to hunt marine mammals.

The approach offered by Daniels is in some ways similar to that used by the Sitka tribe. The Sitka tribe has created by ordinance as an independent entity the Sitka Marine Mammal Commission. This organization issues permits to hunt marine mammals to qualified and enrolled tribal members who meet the MMPA regulatory criteria for Alaska Native. The permit authorizes the person to engage in legal and culturally appropriate marine mammal hunting and usage within the traditional territory (which is spatially) defined by the Sitka tribe. The tribal permit constitutes a kind of "certification" based on review of the qualifications of applicants to be hunters; it only confirms their eligibility if they can demonstrate 1/4 blood quantum.

BIA Enrollment

BIA enrollment according to Alaska BIA enrollment personnel requires a Certificate of Determination of Indian Blood (CDIB). A CDIB or CIB is obtained by submitting an application to the

Bureau of Indian Affairs. The application includes the requirement for submission of birth or death certificates for parents and grandparents. Following evaluation of the documentation, a determination of the blood quantum is made. If the person has Alaska Native ancestry, a BIA CDIB card is issued that has the blood quantum printed on it. Individuals who may have ancestors from different Alaska Native ethnic groups that are identifiable from the documents submitted will have a proportion listed for each ancestral source. For example, someone might be listed as .50 Tlingit and .25 Chugach indicating that one parent was full blood Tlingit and the other half Chugach.

Anyone enrolled by the Alaska BIA with a CDIB is eligible for BIA services, no matter the blood quantum (BIA enrollment office, personal communication, May 8, 2016). BIA enrollment specifies only Alaska Native status. Therefore, it could be an alternative under the "regarded as" language in the regulations as the MMPA eligibility applies only to Alaska Natives and Alaska BIA CDIBs are issued only to those demonstrating Alaska Native ancestry. The BIA CDIB does not systematically identify the tribal membership of an individual, only the ethnic source of the ancestry, i.e. Tlingit, Haida, Yup'ik, Aleut, etc.

The option of using an Alaska Native CDIB card as a certification of eligibility under the MMPA could be accomplished by statutory amendment or regulatory definition change.

Lineal Descendant

As noted in the information above concerning the history of engagement with this issue by Alaska Native organizations, on numerous occasions the concept of lineal descendant or lineal descent has been proposed for determination of Alaska Native eligibility by Alaska Native groups. Under this alternative, lineal descendants of original ANCSA shareholders would be regarded as meeting the MMPA statute and regulatory criteria of Alaska Native. It should be pointed out that "Descendant" was defined by amendment in ANCSA Section 3 (43 U.S.C. 1602) in 1988 to mean: "(1) a lineal descendant of a Native or of an individual who would have been a Native if such individual were alive on December 18, 1971, or (2) an adoptee of a Native or of a descendant of a Native, whose adoption (A) occurred prior to his or her majority, and (B) is recognized at law or in equity." Whether this would meet the statutory definition of Alaska Native for purposes of the MMPA is unclear but would not likely meet the regulatory definition of Alaska Native. Lineal descendants of Alaska Native tribal enrollees would also qualify under this alternative. There are some Alaska Natives who meet BIA enrollment or IHS eligibility criteria who might not qualify.

Language specifying ANCSA shareholder status, Alaska Native tribal membership, or lineal descendancy from an ANCSA shareholder or Alaska Native tribal member could be developed as the definition of Alaska Native for MMPA purposes. It could be incorporated into the statute by amendment, included through rule-making in the regulations, or specified through a "policy statement," an "administrative ruling," or an "understanding" published by the agencies.

Alaska Native Marine Mammal Organizations

Marine mammal co-management organizations and tribal commissions could be considered as alternate institutions to certify Alaska Native eligibility. The MMPA was amended in 1994 in order to establish co-management organizations and regimes. Section 119 of the Marine Mammal Protection Act Amendments of 1994 (Public Law 103-238) granted NMFS and the US Fish and Wildlife Service authority to enter into cooperative agreements with Alaska Native Organizations (ANOs). Agreements may involve: 1) developing marine mammal co-management structures and processes with federal and state agencies, 2) monitoring the harvest of marine mammals for subsistence use, 3) participating in marine mammal research, and 4) collecting and analyzing data on marine mammal populations. The agreements do not include any language concerning powers to consult with agencies in the promulgation of regulations, authority to initiate "rule making" to address criteria for Alaska Native eligibility, or to certify hunters as eligible under the MMPA. The following organizations currently have some form of recognized co-management agreements with NMFS or USFWS:

- Alaska Beluga Whale Committee (ABWC)
- Alaska Eskimo Whaling Commission
- Aleut Marine Mammal Commission
- Alaska Nanuuq Commission
- Alaska Native Harbor Seal Commission (ANHSC)
- Eskimo Walrus Commission
- Ice Seal Committee
- Indigenous People's Council for Marine Mammals (IPCoMM)
- Memorandum of Agreement for Negotiation of Marine Mammal Protection Act Section 119 agreements between the Department of Commerce, the Fish and Wildlife Service, the Geological Survey and the Indigenous People's Council for Marine Mammals
- Traditional Council of St. George Island (fur seals and sea lions)
- Tribal Government of St. Paul (fur seals and sea lions)

In addition, the Cook Inlet Marine Mammal Council (CIMMC) operated under co-management agreements for Cook Inlet beluga whales from 2000-2012. It was disbanded by unanimous vote of the then CIMMC member Tribes' representatives on June 20, 2012.

There are other ANOs that are actively involved in the management of marine mammals that presently do not have co-management agreements with either agency. These include:

- The Alaska Sea Otter and Steller Sea Lion Commission (TASSC) – operates through affiliation with the Alaska Native Harbor Seal Commission.
- Bristol Bay Marine Mammal Council – participates in IPCoMM, ABWC, ANHSC, and TASSC.

- Prince of Wales Tribal Sea Otter Commission – consisting of the tribes of Craig, Hydaburg, Kasaan, and Klawock located on Prince of Wales Island. Self-organized tribal entity with no affiliation.
- Qayassiq Walrus Commission (QWC) – Bristol Bay Native organization that oversees walrus harvesting at Round Island in western Bristol Bay for twelve Bristol Bay tribes that participate in walrus hunting. The QWC completed and signed a cooperative agreement in September 1995 with the Eskimo Walrus Commission, the Alaska Department of Fish & Game, and the US Fish and Wildlife Service.
- Sitka Marine Mammal Commission (SMMC) – an independent management entity authorized by ordinance of the Sitka Tribe of Alaska. As a creation of a tribe, and therefore a tribal entity, the SMMC is the only Alaska Native marine mammal management organization to have an established process for "certifying" the legal eligibility of tribal members to participate in marine mammal harvesting and use. These tribal actions are undertaken as a matter of tribal sovereignty and are not authorized by the MMPA amendments nor are the agencies empowered to enforce the MMPA.

IPCoMM Chair Mike Miller characterizes the SMMC actions as follows:

> Sitka Tribe doesn't allow or not allow anyone to hunt at this time. Sitka Tribe issues permits for identification to Tribal Citizens who meet the listed criteria for the permit. The permit assures L.E. that the holder meets the minimum Federal qualifications and the holder has records on file at [Sitka Tribe of Alaska]. (Miller, personal communication, July 5, 2016)

The SMMC permit is for the hunting of marine mammals only in the traditional territory of the Sitka Tribe which are delineated.

IPCoMM as the umbrella organization created to address similar Alaska Native issues and concerns about marine mammals has been the forum for discussions of the Alaska Native eligibility criteria for nearly a decade. During the discussions, representatives of the various organizations have not been able to come to a unified position. IPCoMM Chair Mike Miller stated that he could recall no discussion of the co-management organizations becoming organizations involved in the determination of eligibility at any time when the issue of Alaska Native criteria determining eligibility has been on the table. Nor has there been any discussion of IPCoMM itself becoming empowered to certify Alaska Native eligibility.

Amendments to the legislation would be required if the co-management institutions were to become the entities responsible for certification of MMPA Alaska Native eligibility.

Alaska Native and Indian Resolutions Addressing the MMPA Regulatory Definition

The specific language and recommendations found in recent ANO and Indian resolutions concerning changes to the MMPA regulatory definition are extracted from the actual resolution document and presented below. The full resolution can be found in the appendices.

> **AFN Resolution – 2009-08**
>
> **NOW THEREFORE BE IT RESOLVED** that the CFR (50 CFR 18) be revised, if required, to allow each Alaska Native Tribe to authorize and allow Alaska Native ANCSA descendants to non-wastefully take, possess, and utilize sea otters for subsistence or handicraft purposes; and
>
> **BE IT FURTHER RESOLVED** that the regulations be further amended to allow Alaska

Native members of Alaska Native tribal governments to non-wastefully take, possess, and utilize sea otters for subsistence and handicraft purposes.

AFN Resolution – 2010-11

NOW THEREFORE BE IT RESOLVED by the Delegates to the 2010 Annual Convention of the Alaska Federation of Natives Inc., that the Alaska Federation of Natives petition the Secretaries of Interior and Commerce to change the definition of "Alaskan Native" under 50 CFR 18.3 and 50 CFR 216.3 to include lineal Alaska Natives descendants of less than one-fourth blood quantum.

[Note: This resolution was directed to the AFN Subsistence Committee which delegated it to IPCoMM for additional review and action.]

NCAI Resolution – 2010-015

NOW THEREFORE BE IT RESOLVED, that the NCAI fully support and advocate for the petition to the Secretaries of Interior and Commerce to change the definition of "Alaskan Native" under 50 CFR 18.3 and 50 CFR 216.3 to include lineal Alaska Natives' descendants of less than one-fourth blood quantum, those originally enrolled in the Alaska Native Claims Settlement Act, and Alaska Natives enrolled in a federally recognized tribal government;

CCTHITA Resolution – 2016-19

NOW THEREFORE BE IT RESOLVED, that the Eighty-First Tribal Assembly of Central Council of Tlingit and Haida Indian Tribes of

> Alaska Delegation convened in Juneau, Alaska on April 20-22, 2016, hereby requests the removal of "blood quantum" in the definition for hunting marine mammals and request this definition be changed to recognize descendancy that could be proven by tribal enrollment cards, BIA Blood Quantum Certificates or other proof of descendancy.

Summation

The three most commonly proposed alternative criteria that Alaska Native commentators and interviewees mentioned to make Alaska Natives of less than 1/4 blood quantum eligible under the MMPA are 1) tribal membership, 2) lineal descendancy from either an ANCSA original shareholder or an Alaskan Native tribal member for those who are not members of such organizations themselves, and 3) CDIB. One commentator, knowledgeable through participation in regional program administration and marine mammal co-management institutions commented that "The majority of the ANOs in rural Alaska that I know of as long as a person is tribally enrolled, they shouldn't have any issues hunting for their grandparents and family." Supporters of the tribal membership alternative emphasize the right of tribes to set the criteria for their own members and therefore tribes that wished to retain a 1/4 blood quantum could do so while others could make their own decisions on whom to include. Views differ on whether tribal members without Alaskan Native ancestry should be eligible to hunt.

In terms of additional Alaska Natives that would be made eligible by the three criteria, CDIB is the most expansive and would include the most individuals, lineal descendancy would be intermediate, and tribal membership would expand the number of hunters the least.

ALASKA NATIVES VIEWS ON MMPA ELIGIBILITY CRITERIA

Study Objective 5. Obtain views of organizational leaders as to the advisability of changing the current regulatory definition of "Alaska Native" and to the suitability of possible alternate criteria for "Alaska Native" under MMPA.

Initially this research objective concerned examination only of the suitability of alternate possible criteria for defining Alaska Native. In the early phases of the research, however, it was determined it was important to obtain the views of Alaska Natives on the advisability of changing the current definition. This would make it possible to examine the full range of views on the definition not merely on what alternate criteria might be suitable.

In order to obtain information needed to meet this objective, several activities were undertaken. Presentations of pertinent information through briefings and PowerPoint slide shows were made to virtually all of the Alaska Native co-management organizations created under the MMPA as well as other Alaska marine mammal organizations and some tribes (see Appendix 2 for list of presentations to groups). Additional interviews were conducted with Alaska Native leaders who have long-term experience with the issue, tribal leaders in hub communities from Ketchikan to Barrow, and with Alaska Native taggers working for the USFWS (see Appendix 3 for list of interviewed persons).

In addition to the presentations and interviews, background documents and information have been acquired and examined on the history of Alaska Native engagement with the issue of MMPA criteria for Alaska Native eligibility. Carol Daniels (2011), former AFN attorney who investigated the MMPA Native eligibility issue, prepared a memorandum to AFN President Julie Kitka in May 2011 that included much of the discussion found below on the history of ANO involvement up to that time.

History of Alaska Native Organizations Addressing the Issue of MMPA Eligibility

The Indigenous People's Council for Marine Mammals (IPCoMM) has been struggling with this issue for a number of years, as have some of the regional non-profits. In 2009, Koniag submitted and the delegates passed AFN Convention Resolution 09-08, which urged the Secretary of the Interior to take immediate and all necessary action to ensure that lineal descendants and Alaska Native tribal members of less than one-fourth blood quantum could continue their subsistence traditions pertaining to sea otter harvest and use [see Appendix 4]. In 2010, Koniag submitted AFN Convention Resolution 10-11, which called upon the Secretaries of Interior and Commerce to change the regulatory definition of "Alaska Native" to include lineal Alaska Native descendants of less than one-fourth blood quantum [see Appendix 5]. The resolution was referred to the AFN Subsistence Workgroup and addressed at some length by the AFN Federal Policy Committee, the Subsistence Workgroup and the AFN Board in subsequent meetings last fall. The AFN Board requested that IPCoMM continue its work on this issue and to make periodic reports to the AFN Federal Policy Committee.

AFN President Julie Kitka sent a letter to IPCoMM Chair Mike Miller in January 2011, requesting the organization continue to "work on the issue" and make "periodic reports" to the AFN Federal Policy Committee. At IPCoMM's March 2011 meeting in Anchorage, the issue was once again raised and discussed. Mike Miller, President, informed the group of AFN's request that IPCoMM take the lead in addressing this issue. Some members expressed the view that this is a tribal issue and one that needs to be addressed more broadly within the Native community. The IPCoMM membership had different views on how best to address the issue – some support a revision to the definition to include lineal descendants and others believed each tribe should be allowed to decide who is eligible for the exemption. IPCoMM ultimately decided to inform AFN that it wished to "remain neutral" on the issue and that AFN should work with the tribal governments to propose a solution.

At its April, 2011, meeting in Kodiak, the Alaska Native Harbor Seal Commission (ANHSC), a member of IPCoMM, voted to send a letter to the Alaska Region, NOAA fisheries, asking NOAA to initiate a review of its definition of "Alaska Native" in light of the impact it is having on Native families across Alaska. The ANHSC asked NOAA to voluntarily initiate rulemaking to amend the definition **so that lineal descendants of Alaska Natives with 1/4 Native blood quanta can participate with their families in the harvest and utilization of marine mammals** [emphasis added]. The NMFS responded that given the broad use of the term and the many agencies involved, both statewide and nationwide, NMFS did not believe it would be appropriate for NMFS to unilaterally initiate changes to the definition. Noting the differing perspectives in the Alaska Native community as to whether any

> change should be made to existing definitions, NMFS encouraged ANHSC to work through IPCoMM as the umbrella organization generally representing Alaska native marine mammal organizations throughout the state. (Daniels 2011)

Not included in the foregoing summary of Alaska Native organization action on MMPA Alaska Native eligibility is the passage by the Kodiak Island Roundtable, a consortium of tribal and corporate entities of the Koniag region, in September 2009, of a resolution entitled "Supporting regulatory changes to allow Tribal Members and/or Alaska Native ANCSA descendants to take, possess, and utilize sea otters for subsistence and handicrafts." This resolution was subsequently forwarded to AFN by Koniag and is resolution 09-08 acted upon by AFN in October 2009.

In November 2010, the National Congress of American Indians passed resolution #ABQ-10-015 entitled "The Protection and Continuation of Customary and Traditional Practices for Marine Mammal Subsistence for Future Generations" [see Appendix 6]. The resolution requested the Secretaries of Commerce and Interior to address the MMPA regulatory definition of Alaska Native and to change the definition of "Alaskan Native" under 50 CFR 18.3 and 50 CFR 216.3 to "include lineal Alaska Native descendants of less than one-fourth blood quantum, those originally enrolled in the Alaska Native Claims Settlement Act, and Alaska Natives enrolled in a federally recognized tribal government."

In 2014, the Chugach Rural Resources Council (CRRC), representing the tribes of the Chugach region, requested and obtained a meeting with USFWS administrator Geoff Haskett to discuss the issue of the MMPA criteria for Alaska Native eligibility. The meeting was also attended by Mike Miller and Peggy Osterback of IPCoMM. Haskett informed the group that it was important for his agency and NMFS to receive the views of Alaska Natives on the issue. He further indicated that he would coordinate with his NMFS counterpart to send a letter to IPCoMM indicating the agency's desire to hear the views of the affected Alaska Native community on the issue.

In a letter to IPCoMM and AFN dated October 10, 2014, Jon Kurland of NMFS and Timothy Jenkins of the USFWS wrote (see Appendix 8):

> The FWS has been contacted by several Tribal Governments, expressing concern that the current regulatory definition may be too limiting to Tribes and their members. The FWS and NMFS recognize that both the Indigenous People's Council on Marine Mammals (IPCoMM) and the Alaska Federation of Natives (AFN) have vested interest in subsistence related regulatory definitions. As such we request that IPCoMM and AFN's Subsistence Committee review the current regulatory definitions and advise FWS and NMFS as to whether your respective organizations believe a change is needed. If a change is warranted, please identify in your comments what should be addressed, and if you desire, propose specific language you would like us to consider. Any change could affect the way subsistence harvests are conducted and managed, so if you do support consideration of a change, we would be interested in your thoughts as to how best to proceed so that all affected stakeholders can participate in that process.

The most recent formal organizational action on this issue was taken by the Central Council of the Tlingit and Haida Indian Tribes of Alaska who at their annual convention in April 2016, passed resolution TA/16-19 entitled "In Support of Changing the Definition of Blood Quantum in the Marine Mammal Regulations to Descendancy" (see Appendix 9). The specific language in the resolution dealing with the request for changed criteria is that CCTHITA "hereby requests the removal of 'blood quantum' in the definition for hunting marine mammals and request this definition be changed to recognize descendancy that could be proven by tribal enrollment cards, BIA Blood Quantum Certificates, or other proof of descendancy."

In March 2016, an amendment to the MMPA (S. 2728, the "Alaska Native Access Card Act") was introduced by Alaska US Senator Dan Sullivan at the request of the Arctic Slope Regional Corporation. The purpose of the bill is to facilitate the import of marine mammal products into the United States by Alaska Natives. The original language included the incorporation of the MMPA regulatory definition of Alaska Native into the act. A number of ANOs expressed concern to Senator Sullivan's office concerning the proposed language that would import the MMPA regulatory definition into the law. Senator Sullivan's office called for input from the larger Alaska Native community on the definition question. Subsequently ASRC circulated a memo identifying five "options for including a definition of the term 'Alaska Native'" in the MMPA. The five options proposed were as follows:

1. Amend the MMPA to define the term "Alaska Native" in a manner that includes "Descendants" – as defined in ANCSA.
2. Amend the MMPA to define as separate terms, "Alaska Native" and "Descendant of a Native," and utilize the terms as appropriate throughout the MMPA.
3. Eliminate use of definitions that depend upon a "Blood Quantum" threshold, and define the term "Alaska Native" by reference to membership in an "Indian Tribe" as defined by the Indian Self Determination Act and Education Assistance Act.
4. Amend the MMPA to define the term "Alaska Native" using a definition similar to that used in ANCSA as well as in existing MMPA regulations; explore options for amending the definition through the legislative process
5. Do not amend the MMPA to define the term "Alaska Native."

The full text of the memorandum discussing each option at greater length is found in Appendix 10 of this report. While circulated to a number of Alaska Native leaders involved with the MMPA Native eligibility issue, these options have not been the subject of discussion before any Alaska Native organization as of this writing.

Alaska Native Views on MMPA Regulatory Definition of Alaska Native

This section discusses views of Alaska Natives as given during presentations to organizations and in individual interviews. An information advisory handout was provided to board or council members at meetings to be used to explore the issue and various options. While it was clear that members of co-management boards were familiar with the issue, this was often not the case for tribal council members, especially those new to their duties. In discussions at organizational meetings, different perspectives were often offered by various members of the boards.

It should be asserted at the outset that virtually all Alaska Natives wish to see the exemption for Alaska Natives maintained and that they are extremely concerned about the 1/4 blood quantum gradually dividing the population, creating unwanted divisiveness, increasing anxiety about enforcement actions, and the "chilling" effect of potential criminalization of families passing on their traditional values and practices to descendants of less than 1/4 blood quantum. Commentators at co-management meetings where information on the MMPA Alaska Native eligibility issue was presented for discussion observed that the topic "opens up a can of worms" and that "it stirs things up." The issue continues to be unsettling and discomforting for many reasons.

During the course of this research in many communities and on a number of occasions, the views of young Alaska Natives on being excluded from hunting marine mammals were transmitted to me, often through their parents or grandparents. One commentator who works in a Native organization noted that nearly every week one of the younger Native employees less than 1/4 would comment on the unfairness that their blood quantum denies them rights as a full-fledged shareholder and eligibility to hunt marine mammals. It has been pointed out by several commentators that there is no forum for younger people to express themselves on the issue and many feel that they cannot even enter the debate without risk of being criminalized.

Contexts

While the topic of the MMPA Alaska Native criteria for eligibility was the primary focus of discussion, a number of other considerations often entered the discussion quickly. These can be referred to as the contexts in which deliberation on this issue will be conducted.

Alaska Native Exemption. Rights of Alaska Natives, as the indigenous people of Alaska, to the customary and traditional use of resources (subsistence) was a significant backdrop issue. Commentators noted that ANCSA extinguished aboriginal fishing and hunting rights without consulting with or informing Alaska Natives of the inclusion of that provision in the final form of ANCSA. However, in the "conference report accompanying ANCSA… Congress expressed the clear intention that Alaska Native subsistence interests (hunting, fishing, trapping, and gathering) should be protected by the Secretary of the Interior and the state of Alaska" (Case and Voluck 2015: 291). More specifically, the report stipulated that the Secretary and the State of Alaska were "to take any action necessary to protect the subsistence needs of the Natives" (Case and Voluck 2015: 292).

Arising from Title (d) (2) of ANCSA, Title 8 of the Alaska National Interest Lands Conservation Act (ANILCA), passed in 1980, addressed the issue of subsistence uses in Alaska. The law makes a distinction between "rural" and "urban" communities based on population size and cultural characteristics. It establishes a "rural preference" for subsistence uses which while distinguishing Alaska Native "cultural" bases from non-Native "social" bases, provides the preference equally to rural Native and non-Native residents. It has been suggested that Alaska Natives were parties to this outcome by "trad[ing] their support for ANILCA's environmentally oriented land classifications for environmentalist support of ANILCA's title VIII subsistence provisions" (Case and Voluck 2015: 296). According to Case and Voluck (2015: 296):

> By its terms, title VIII of ANILCA is intended to carry out the subsistence-related policies and fulfill the purposes of ANCSA. In this respect, it is in some sense a settlement of Alaska Native aboriginal hunting and fishing claims, seemingly extinguished in ANCSA.

For some Alaska Native commentators, this act represents a significant departure from the subsistence rights of Alaska Natives as the indigenous occupants of Alaska as extinguished by ANCSA and they view the ANILCA regime as a substantial diminishment of those rights. The loss of subsistence rights by non-rural Alaska Natives and lack of Alaska Native subsistence rights on state lands are two concerns pointed to by Native commentators. These concerns have been the basis of recurrent efforts through the AFN Subsistence Committee by some Alaska Natives to seek an amendment or legislation that would provide a subsistence priority for Alaska Natives no matter the location of their residence and without regard to the lands/waters on which they are exercising those rights.

Another problematic case of the treatment of Alaska Natives subsistence rights that was brought up by commentators is the situation of migratory bird treaty and protocol definitions and rules concerning subsistence uses. Migratory bird treaties from the early 20th century to which the United States was a party outlawed the customary and traditional harvests of birds and eggs by Alaska Natives through the closing of the hunting season between March 10 and September 1. The attempted enforcement of the ban on Alaska Native harvests that was undertaken by USFWS in the early 1960s electrified

Native users who often for the first time were confronted with governmental efforts to halt customary and traditional subsistence harvests. In Barrow, the Iñupiat community staged the famous Duck-In to protest the citing of an Iñupiat hunter for taking ducks and asserted their subsistence rights based on tradition and customary use. Subsequently, in 1978 the United States amended the Migratory Bird Treaty Act to allow adoption of regulations authorizing the harvest of migratory birds. The United States negotiated new treaties and protocols that generally provided for the harvest of migratory waterfowl but under slightly different regimes. Efforts have been made by the federal government to create a unified system of law and regulation concerning the taking of migratory birds. In 2002, the Alaska Migratory Bird Co-Management Council was created, which proposes annual subsistence harvest regulations. At issue for Alaska Native commentators and users is the following language found in the 1997 protocol to the treaty between the US and Mexico, which was necessary to authorize migratory bird taking:

> ...in the state of Alaska, United States of America, where wild ducks and their eggs may be harvested by indigenous inhabitants thereof provided that seasons and other regulations implementing the non-wasteful taking of wild ducks and their eggs in such cases shall be consistent with the customary and traditional uses by such indigenous inhabitants for their own nutritional and other essential needs.

In 1998, the USFWS stated, "The United States understands that the term 'indigenous inhabitants' means a permanent resident of a village within the subsistence harvest area, regardless of race" (Case and Voluck 2015: 273). New regulations, 50 CFR Part 92 authorizing harvests defined "Indigenous inhabitant" as a "permanent resident of a village within a subsistence harvest area, regardless of race." In subsequent actions, non-Native residents of "subsistence harvest areas" have been considered legal users of migratory birds by the USFWS.

For Alaska Native commentators, this redefinition of "indigenous" to mean "permanent resident…regardless of race" represents another diminishment of Alaska Native subsistence rights.

The underlying concern of Alaska Native commentators pointing to these outcomes is that there is a substantial danger that efforts to change the MMPA regulatory definition of Alaska Native could result in the loss of the blanket Alaska Native exemption that is presently in place or any kind of Alaska Native preference. At present, all coastally resident Alaska Natives can harvest marine mammals but the regimes of ANILCA both eliminate non-rural Natives while allowing rural non-Native participation in customary and traditional Alaska Native subsistence activities. Either of these results, loss of the exemption or modification of the exemption to a regime similar to ANILCA, are seen as extremely problematic and detrimental to Alaska Natives. It should be noted that the MMPA's present blanket exemption for all species in all regions is seen by many Alaska Native commentators as fraught with problems as well due to its failure to recognize regional cultural traditions and patterns of use which many Alaska Natives see as the foundation for their use of marine mammals.

It is noteworthy that assimilation of the MMPA regime of Alaska Native eligibility currently in place to one similar to ANILCA could well result in the loss of rights of non-rural Alaska Natives to hunt marine mammals. Thus Alaska Native residents of Anchorage, Juneau, the Kenai area, and Ketchikan who are currently eligible to harvest marine mammals under MMPA statutory language could be deemed ineligible.

Increasing Bureaucratization. Commentators pointed out that the MMPA and the regulations through which it is operationalized are presently quite light in the bureaucratic burden that is imposed on Alaska Native marine mammal hunters. However, uncertainty about standards as to what constitute "traditional manufacturers of handicrafts" creates substantial anxiety and fear of violation resulting in prosecution for many involved in the creation of traditional handicrafts. No permit or license is required to hunt or manufacture.

Identification when hunting marine mammals is not required. With the exception of sea otter, polar bear, and walrus, harvesters do not have to report to agencies on the number, location, or any other data on harvested marine mammals. Bowhead whales are managed through a separate cooperative agreement between the Alaska Eskimo Whaling Commission and the Department of Commerce that has proved to be successful. Commentators are concerned that change, especially formal efforts to change the MMPA Native eligibility criteria, will set in motion additional regulatory action by agencies that will increase the burden on Alaska Native hunting and using marine mammals. There is currently substantial resistance by a number of Alaska Natives to requirements to obtain permits for migratory bird harvesting. Impasse over these provisions has prevented the establishment of new regulations for the harvesting of Emperor geese (Fall, personal communication, July 13, 2016). There could emerge other agency-initiated forms of unanticipated regulatory change that might also negatively impact how Alaska Natives currently utilize marine mammals.

Alaska Native commentators who provided observations on contexts of the effort to change the MMPA regulatory criteria did not necessarily have views on the benefits of or the impacts of changes if they could be accomplished without consequences for the Alaska Native exemption or the current regulatory regime regarding permits, reporting, and harvest levels. They may either support or oppose certain types of changes to the criteria used in the regulatory definition. Their emphasis is on the inherent danger of entering into efforts to effect changes agreed to by Alaska Natives when the process and outcomes might be deleterious and there is little assurance as to what that outcome might be.

Biological Status of Stocks. A number of commentators raised the question of the current biological status of various species and what effect changing the criteria and making more hunters eligible to harvest those species might mean. Since 2008, seven arctic marine species have been listed as threatened, endangered, or classified as species of concern under the US Endangered Species Act, virtually all due to climate change. Commentators who raised this issue indicated that it was important to consider both the status of the species and its stocks, especially those that Alaska Native groups depend on for survival.

Supporters of Criteria Change

Supporters of changes to the MMPA regulatory definition have made their case on multiple occasions through requests to agencies for regulatory changes and through resolutions of their organizations. In those materials, supporters of criteria change assert several arguments. These positions can be categorized as legal, moral, and cultural.

Legal Arguments. There are three arguments under this category that have been used.

1) The regulatory definition in the MMPA is not consistent with language of the law and is more restrictive than the law. They contend that there is nothing in the legislative history of the MMPA that indicates Congress intended to limit the exemption to Alaska Natives who are 1/4 or more Alaska Native ancestry. Another point of inconsistency noted between language in the statute and the regulatory definition is that the statute in using the term "Indian" does not explicitly identify Alaskan Indians and therefore can be read that the exemption applies to any Indian or Native American who resides on the coast of Alaska. The regulations by contrast stipulate Alaskan Indian as stated in the ANCSA definition.

2) The regulatory definition in the MMPA does not promote the purpose of the exemption to make possible the preservation and handing down of cultural traditions and cultural "way of life" as called for by the legislative history of the act. Congress conducted hearings in Bethel and Nome in 1972 on the basis of which the report notes:

> The findings were that most villages of northern Alaska depend upon marine mammals not only for food, clothing and implements, but utilize products

> from seals, whales and walruses as the basis for their small cash economy. An Eskimo hunter may bring in a seal, which is cut up for food, pelt and seal oil. Any excess beyond family needs can be sold to neighbors or turned in at a village store for credit on gasoline, fuel oil or ammunition.

Supporters similarly cite US Senator Ted Stevens's justification from the legislative history that the exemption was necessary in order for cultural practices to be passed down from generation to generation. Additionally, the testimony of US Senator Fritz Hollings during floor debate on the MMPA is cited in which he stated:

> Native Alaskans are proud. They do not ask for special treatment from the Federal Government. But, nonetheless, they, too, have the right to be left alone, to follow their traditional way of life. ***It is this way of life I seek to protect in this bill. ...*** [emphasis added]
>
> Alaskan arts and crafts are an artistic and social heritage. This skill, handed down from generation to generation, reveals as much of their history as paintings Rembrandt and other famous European artists reveals of the white man's past history. ***Removing the privilege of passing this cultural legacy to future generations will sever children as yet unborn from the past. It will create a cultural Diaspora.*** [emphasis added]

These statements are presented by those supporting criteria change as evidence of Congressional intent to allow for the transmission of the Alaska Native way of life from generation to generation.

3) The application of the regulation is not fully implemented since there is no operationalization of the section of the regulation that stipulates that "in the absence of proof of blood quantum..." those

"regarded as…" are to be considered Alaska Natives. One commentator observed that the agencies in their own regulatory definition have the tools to address the issue through the "regarded as…" provision but have chosen not to. It was further observed that Alaska Natives should not have to be proactive on the issue as it is incumbent on agencies to provide for full implementation of their regulations. A non-Alaska Native commentator who worked for years for a co-management institution stated that "It is as though, for all practical purposes, this clause doesn't exist."

Moral Arguments. Four types of positions for changing the criteria that can be classified as moral in nature follow.

1) Certain Alaska Native communities are dependent on marine mammals for a substantial part of their foods. Others depend heavily on the money obtained from the sale of handicrafts made out of marine mammal materials. If communities are to survive then younger members, some of whom may be less than 1/4 blood quantum, must be able to provide for their grandparents, parents, and themselves. It is morally right to allow people of less than 1/4 blood quantum to hunt to provide for their communities. It is morally wrong to deny such persons the right to hunt and provide for their families and community.

2) Proponents of changing the criteria assert that all families, as a matter of human rights, have the right to transmit their cultural heritage to their descendants, regardless of governmental and legal positions. A number of commentators at presentations made this point in various fashions, some vehemently.

3) Another form of this argument is that it is not fair for some descendants of Alaska Natives to be eligible under the MMPA and others not. Commentators note that the genealogical paperwork necessary to document 1/4 blood quantum is not available uniformly to all Alaska Natives due to a number of factors. The paperwork that is available is also problematically being based on unfairness. Several Alaska Native elders noted that they have some grandchildren who are eligible and some who are not eligible. This is very disturbing and

painful for them. To them, it is not fair for some of their descendants to be ineligible to hunt marine mammals, which is so central to cultural identity and the maintenance of cultural traditions.

4) The supporters of changing the criteria note several critical deleterious impacts and implications of MMPA enforcement of the regulatory definition of Alaska Native. A White Paper (see Appendix 7) on the necessity of changing the Alaska Native eligibility criteria prepared by the Alaska Sea Otter and Sea Lion Commission in 2010 stated that:

> In our communities, there are children who do not meet the minimum blood quantum, yet their parents, grandparents and other family members continue their traditional and customary practices including marine mammal hunting and sewing. This is harming our communities. Our traditions are in danger of being lost, or our members are made to feel like criminals and fear prosecution for teaching their kids.

Possible prosecution for teaching children and grandchildren cultural practices and traditions handed down for generations could result from the enforcement of the current regulatory definition of an Alaska Native.

Cultural Arguments. Two kinds of positions using cultural propositions have been offered for changing the criteria.

1) Many Alaska Natives believe that their cultural practices are transmitted by parents and relatives to their descendants in the context of communities. It is a right, an obligation, and a practice. The values and practices of the culture are transmitted to all young people in the community. Through exposure to the teachings of Elders, the examples of leaders, and the observation of appropriate behaviors and practices, young people come to a realization of what they are to do and how they are to behave. Another way of putting this realization as a result of such training and exposure is that one comes to see who they are and what they should do. It is not possible and it is deeply damaging

to deny certain children and grandchildren the right to grow up as full members of their communities.

2) Cultural traditions as a way of life are a totality and it is fundamentally wrong to separate one part of that tradition from others. Young Alaska Natives of less than 1/4 blood quantum in coastal villages are able to hunt migratory birds and collect their eggs and they are able to hunt sheep, goats, moose, deer, and elk, and they are able to trap mink, marten, land otter, and other furbearers, but they are not allowed to hunt marine mammals or utilize marine mammal parts. This is both injurious and nonsensical.

Supporters of No Criteria Change

Alaska Natives who are generally in favor of not changing the criteria fall into two camps. The first camp considers that given the contexts of pursuing change that might lead to loss or substantial modification of the Alaska Native exemption, it is unwise and even dangerous to formally pursue change. The second camp who generally favor the current situation advanced arguments in four areas. These can be classified as imbalance, biological, management, and cultural.

Imbalance Arguments. Imbalance arguments are offered as follows:

1) The change in the criteria would dramatically increase the number of eligible hunters. This would likely result in additional harvests and those additional harvests would be at the expense of those already taking the marine mammals who depend on them. This would increase the competition for scarce resources that current hunters are presently in need of. This comment was made in regard to sea otter harvests in southeast Alaska.

2) The livelihoods of Alaska Natives who depend on the creation and sale of traditional handicrafts would be severely damaged, or perhaps even lost. One commentator dependent for income on making handicrafts from marine mammal materials stated that markets for the objects created would soon be flooded and expected that income would be dramatically reduced. The danger of changing the criteria to allow

those of less than 1/4 blood quantum was so great to the disruption of the present circumstances of those dependent on marine mammals for their economic livelihood that one commentator was comfortable with the fact that several grandchildren of the commentator were ineligible to harvest or use marine mammals.

Biological Arguments. The basic claim of the biological justification for maintenance of the status quo is that changing the criteria would increase the number of hunters which would result in increased harvests of certain marine mammals. This could lead to overharvesting. This would then precipitate limitations on the harvests of present hunters who are providing for their communities and households. It could even lead to closure of hunting or implementation of regulations on seasons and bag limits. These closures would threaten community survival not to mention the survival of cultural traditions.

Management Arguments. The management concern of those opposed to changing the criteria is that it will become significantly more difficult for enforcement agents to identify who is an Alaska Native if the 1/4 blood quantum is reduced. Many ineligible non-Natives will attempt to hunt marine mammals and Alaska Natives will have to carry their identification papers and respond to more frequent requests from enforcement to prove their status. It would be even more difficult for manufacturers of handicrafts from marine mammal products as there is much less opportunity for oversight of that activity due to the difficulty of linking an object crafted to its producer.

Cultural Arguments. Commentators at a number of presentations made the argument that what was at stake was the continuity of critical relationships between humans and marine mammals that was at the heart of cultural beliefs and traditions. Put another way, hunting marine mammals "puts in motion a set of social relations with animals, kin, and the environment that, in their sum, define what it is to be a real human being" (Voorhees 2015). In this view, characterized as "relational sustainability," what is crucial to the existence of both humans and marine mammals is respectful actions by humans, the result of which will be the reproduction of the marine mammals and their future return to give themselves to those who have conducted their relations appropriately. Persons who are not raised in the appropriate cultural context with the appropriate cultural values threaten everyone by their potentially disrespectful behavior toward the marine mammals. One inappropriate type of behavior is reducing the relationship to one of obtaining money and not fully utilizing the animal that has given itself to the hunter. On St. Lawrence Island, the Siberian Yupik tribes have codified these requirements for tribal members hunting of walrus for full utilization and respectful treatment. The Sitka Marine Mammal Commission similarly requires as part of the permitting process for hunters to affirm that they will hunt in a "culturally appropriate" manner which includes the requirement for full utilization. It is the view of some Alaska Native commentators that those involved in the harvest and use of marine mammals must exhibit the appropriate cultural values and behaviors or the animals will withdraw and be unavailable. This is seen as dependent upon being raised in an environment in which traditional Native values are taught and practiced.

Traditional Native values are most likely to be transmitted when there is an Alaska Native who exhibits traditional values in the daily life of their descendants or other young people on a regular basis. Distance from actual parental and grandparental sources of traditional values and behaviors "dilutes" the cultural understandings due to their lack of available demonstration to the children. To this point, it should be noted that a person of 1/8 blood quantum has only one great-grandparent as the source of their ancestry while a person of 1/16 blood quantum has only one great-great-grandparent. In such cases, the direct transmission of traditional Native cultural values through persons in contact is substantially reduced. For these commentators, mere biological qualification by blood quantum is regarded as unsatisfactory and virtually irrelevant to the cultural requirements for being Native. As one knowledgeable commentator noted, "There are those who are eligible to be Natives but are not considered Native."

Underlying this remark is the cultural premise that Native status and recognition is the result of exposure to traditional cultural values and behaviors of hunting and the demonstration of the appropriate values and behaviors in a community context. And those in turn are most likely to be performed if they have been inculcated from birth or childhood. The sense of identity and its association with marine mammal hunting is especially strong in northwest Alaska where utilization of large marine mammals is critical as data presented previously demonstrated. A recent study paraphrased a longtime Kivalina (an Iñupiat community considered at risk due to vulnerability to increased damage due to climate change) resident as follows:

> When... asked why her people don't move—somewhere, anywhere to be safe—she is polite but firm. The land and the water make the Iñupiat who they are. If they moved to Kotzebue, they would be visitors. Moving to Anchorage or Fairbanks, she said, "would be like asking us not to be a people anymore." (Hamilton et al 2016:14)

Voorhees (2015:5) who worked with the Nanuuq Commission and hunters between 2010 and 2014 asserts:

> There is a very different way of understanding how hunting relates to being Alaska Native. This is the view more commonly held by the hunters themselves. In this view, one *becomes* Siberian Yupik, Inupiaq, or Yup'ik...through hunting. The view that one acquires social identity [and cultural legitimacy] through hunting is nothing new.

The identity created by the complex of social and cultural practices associated with marine mammal hunting is deeply held and those who demonstrate commitment to its totality are highly respected in the indigenous communities of western and northwestern Alaska.

Opponents of criteria change nevertheless expressed dissatisfaction with other aspects of the current MMPA regulatory regime. The major concern was the blanket exemption for Alaska Natives that allows a qualifying coastal resident Alaska Native to hunt any marine mammal anywhere in Alaska. One commentator pointed out that the relocation of Alaska Natives from other regions where beluga whales were utilized as an important subsistence species to Anchorage was a significant factor in the reduction of the Cook Inlet beluga population leading to its placement on the endangered species list in 2008. Another commentator remarked that the recent harvest of a polar bear by an Alaska Native who moved to the North Slope in order to be eligible to hunt them was extremely disturbing to Iñupiat hunters of the region. That a person could do this because they met the criteria for Alaska Native was seen as illegitimate as the person had not been raised in the community or accepted as a member of the Barrow tribe.

A second observation made by commentators at several presentations from three different communities was that tribes should have the power to authorize marine mammal hunting by non-Natives for certain species in their customary and traditional territory who are married to Alaska Native women from the community and are providing for their families through their hunting. The position for local determination of eligibility to hunt marine mammals was also advocated by western Alaska Natives in hearings about the potential transfer of jurisdiction over marine mammals to the State of Alaska held in 1985 (Langdon 1989). It should be noted that tribal constitutions allow for non-Native individuals to be adopted into the tribe if they meet certain cultural and residency requirements. The Sitka Tribal Constitution, for example, stipulates that persons who have demonstrated "social and cultural connections" to the tribe can be enrolled, but that is done on a case-by-case basis. However, as noted earlier, federal courts have ruled that such adoptions do not change the status of the non-Native for purposes of eligibility for federal programs for Indians or Alaska Natives.

Summation

Virtually all Alaska Natives wish to see the Alaska Native exemption in the MMPA retained. Most Alaska Natives would like to see a change in the MMPA regulatory definition that eliminates blood quantum as a criterion. Some Alaska Natives support movement to criteria based on lineal descendancy from tribal members or original ANCSA enrolled shareholders. Other Alaska Natives support movement that would allow tribes to determine who is eligible for the exemption. Alaska Natives are aware that changing the MMPA regulatory criteria is likely not a simple straightforward process but rather would have to be undertaken in contexts that may make it difficult or impossible to achieve the outcome desired by Alaska Natives.

CURRENT ENFORCEMENT OF MMPA ALASKA NATIVE ELIGIBILITY REQUIREMENTS

Study Objective 6. Identify current circumstances in regard to enforcement of blood quantum standard on Alaska Native harvest activities of marine mammals.

The federal agencies with responsibility for enforcement of the provisions of the MMPA are the NMFS and USFWS. The law stipulates that no permit is required for the legal harvesting of marine mammals by Alaska Natives. Agencies as discussed earlier are responsible for different species. For purposes of this discussion, enforcement includes any interactions between agency officials, associates (taggers), and Alaska Native hunters or handicraft manufacturers related to harvesting of marine mammals or their use in manufacturing handicrafts. Responsible parties include tagging program officers, taggers, enforcement field officers, and federal lawyers who are involved in the prosecution of MMPA violations or dealing with other legal questions. Information from interviews with personnel from each of the agencies is provided below.

National Marine Fisheries Service

Jon Kurland of the NMFS Protected Resources Division in Juneau stated in an interview that enforcement agents do not, as a matter of normal procedure, request documents from Alaska Natives or others they encounter hunting marine mammals to prove their eligibility. He noted that there is no requirement in the law for a permit. However, he commented that enforcement officers have the responsibility and freedom to investigate any situation that might be a violation of the MMPA. NMFS uses the 1/4 blood quantum as the criteria of Alaska Native eligibility. In response to a question concerning the "regarded as" provision of the definition of Alaska Native in the regulation, Kurland (email April 28, 2013) replied, "We have no interpretive guidance on this beyond the language in the regulation." He then went on: "As I said before, NMFS assesses these situations on a case-by-case basis as the need arises. That's all."

Enforcement. In conducting enforcement actions concerning Alaska Native eligibility, an NMFS enforcement officer interviewed stated that they utilize the 1/4 blood quantum criteria. The officer stated that there is no ongoing, systematic practice of asking individual hunters to verify their Alaska Native status. In most communities they are familiar with the hunters. If they see someone with a marine mammal in their skiff or with them at the dock that they don't know, they will ask the person about the marine mammal. Normally, the person will answer that they are Alaska Native. They may produce appropriate ID, but if not, the officer requests the person's name and that of their parents, as well as contact information. Then the officer will follow up with an investigation of the person's status.

The officer has never identified an Alaska Native of less than 1/4 blood quantum during an inquiry of this kind. To his knowledge, based on 14 years of experience, no Native of less than 1/4 blood quantum has been cited or prosecuted for harvesting a marine mammal.

Prosecution. Attorney Elisha Falberg of the Enforcement Section of the NMFS Alaska Section was present at my presentation of the issue at the Bristol Bay Marine Mammal Commission. In a later conversation after checking records in her office, she reported that she had never heard of or identified prosecution of an Alaska Native of less than 1/4 blood quantum for a violation of the MMPA in either harvesting activities (taking or "furthering") or sale of "significantly altered" handicraft nor had any other attorneys in her office with whom she discussed the question.

When asked what definition and criteria for Alaska Native NMFS currently used, Falberg stipulated that it was 1/4 blood quantum as found in the regulations. Further inquiry revealed that Falberg was aware of the "regarded as" language in the regulatory criteria. However, she went on to state that she, as well as other attorneys in her section, "had no guidance" on the language.

US Fish and Wildlife Service

Charles Hamilton, administrative specialist with the Fish and Wildlife Service in Anchorage, stated that the agency uses the 1/4 blood quantum criteria for Alaska Natives that is in the regulation. He was not familiar with how enforcement agents interacted with Alaska Native marine mammal hunters. The three marine mammal species that USFWS has jurisdiction over are polar bear, sea otter, and walrus. For a variety of reasons, each of these species (polar bear, sea otter, walrus) has to be tagged after harvesting. Therefore, there are special enforcement activities pertaining to these animals that are different from the other marine mammals under NMFS jurisdiction.

Tagging. The MMPA requires that all sea otter and polar bear hides and skulls and all walrus tusks be tagged by a representative of the US Fish and Wildlife Service. In order to meet this requirement, the Marking, Tagging, and Reporting Program (MTRP) was initiated in 1978. This program is implemented through resident MTRP taggers located in coastal villages and communities throughout Alaska. There are more than 150 taggers located in about 100 villages. Taggers are often Alaska Natives living in one of the coastal communities. According to Brad Benter, head of the USFWS tagging program, most taggers receive direct face-to-face training about how to carry out their tagging responsibilities. In rare cases, a tagger may initially receive only telephone training if there is another local tagger who can provide hands-on instruction. Taggers' instruction from enforcement agents includes providing information that eligible Alaska Native hunters must be at least 1/4 blood quantum. In addition, they are instructed that they are not required to verify the Alaska Native credentials of those seeking their services.

Benter explained that the biological information on removals was the primary focus of his section. Taggers are not directly involved in determining the eligibility of the hunters. That responsibility lies with the enforcement section.

Interviews with two taggers, each with over 10 years of experience, revealed that they have the option of either tagging or not when they are approached by persons with animals that must be tagged. They were told to use their best judgment concerning the Alaska Native eligibility of the person. Both indicated that in certain circumstances they may ask for papers certifying that the hunter meets the criteria of Alaska Native. This would be done if they are not familiar with the person. When carrying out their tagging activities, taggers use a form specifying information about the animal and the hunter (see Appendix 11). Hunter information on the forms includes among other things name, community, and location of harvest. Hunters and the taggers are both required to sign the form. The form does not ask for a Native corporation number or a CDIB card. Nor is there language that asks the hunter or tagger to stipulate by signature that they are eligible under MMPA regulatory criteria for Alaska Natives. Taggers reported that program leader Benter informed them they are not liable if it is determined that a person they certified does not meet the eligibility criteria. One tagger stated that he told the hunters that the burden was on them in regard to their eligibility when they signed the tagging document. One tagger who had tagged 1,200-1,500 otters over the past 10-12 years said that the issue of Alaska Native eligibility had come up once. He had tagged a sea otter for a man who had tribal paperwork but told the tagger he was less than 1/4. Other taggers had refused to carry out the process for him. Another interviewee had tagged over 3,000 sea otters since 1992 and believed he had never tagged for a person of less than 1/4. He would ask for papers showing eligibility only when he was not familiar with a person. He would ask first if the hunter was a shareholder. Virtually every person met this criterion but if not, then he would request other proof such as BIA or tribal enrollment evidence.

Benter stated that he was occasionally approached when in villages about the requirements and has on occasion found Alaska Natives who were not aware of the legality of their harvesting marine mammals. Due to the sensitivity of the topic, he said in recent years he had not brought up the 1/4 blood quantum requirement in such discussions.

Benter stated that it is rare that there is any coordination between his program and that of enforcement. Enforcement officials do not receive copies of any of the polar bear, sea otter, or walrus tags that are sent to their office. However, if they request the information, they will provide them with it. He and the taggers are never part of any prosecution of MMPA violations.

Enforcement. The US Fish and Wildlife enforcement officer interviewed stated that the agency used only the 1/4 blood quantum criteria. Further, individuals who inquire about their eligibility to hunt are told that 1/4 blood quantum is the criteria. He stated he was once approached by a man who said he was 1/4 and wanted to know if his son, who was 1/8, could hunt – the officer stated he told the man that the son was ineligible. The officer reported the man expressed strong dissatisfaction with the situation.

The officer stated that since the law does not require a permit, they do not seek information from hunters about their Alaska Native status unless they are unfamiliar with the person. He had never heard of nor participated in the citing of a person of less than 1/4 blood quantum for harvesting or utilizing marine mammals. There had been cases of citing and prosecuting non-Natives for taking and/or use of marine mammals.

Prosecution. Ken Lord of the US Attorney's Office was interviewed about the prosecution of MMPA violations which are reported to his office by US Fish and Wildlife Agents. He has worked in the division for 16 years. During that time there have been no prosecutions for Alaska Natives of less than 1/4 blood quantum taking marine mammals. There have been numerous prosecutions of non-Natives for willful, as opposed to accidental or incidental, harvesting of marine mammals. Because each violation is handled on a case-by-case basis, he had no way of determining if such a case would be of a civil or criminal nature.

Summation

Both NMFS and USFWS enforcement agents presently use the 1/4 blood quantum MMPA eligibility criteria. They communicate this to interested parties who inquire what the criteria is. They do not systematically approach marine mammal hunters to determine their eligibility but will do so if there are circumstances that warrant it. In addition, further information on the extent of the regulatory impact on other activities related to marine mammals such as handicraft manufacturing and "furthering" (assisting) hunting activities are also routinely conveyed to non-Natives or Natives. Enforcement agents have been approached by Alaska Natives who informed them they were less than 1/4 blood quantum and the agents then told them they were ineligible to hunt or otherwise be involved in the harvest of marine mammals or the manufacture of handicrafts from marine mammal parts. According to attorneys for both agencies, there is no record of any Alaska Native of less than 1/4 blood quantum ever having been cited or prosecuted for violating the MMPA regulation on that basis. There is an awareness by personnel in both agencies that the MMPA regulatory definition of Alaska Native includes a provision for determining who is an Alaska Native when a person is less than 1/4 blood quantum and that no action has been taken to implement that language.

CONCLUSION

Marine mammals have been utilized by coastal Alaska Natives for thousands of years. In 1972, the federal government passed the Marine Mammal Protection Act essentially halting the taking of marine mammals. Alaska Natives living in coastal communities lobbied for and received an exemption from the general prohibition in recognition of their dependence on marine mammals for physical and cultural survival. Jurisdiction for implementing the act was delegated to the National Marine Fisheries Service and the US Fish and Wildlife Service. The regulatory definition of Alaska Native adopted by the agencies, modeled on the definition of Alaska Native found in the Alaska Native Claims Settlement Act of 1971, specified that an Alaska Native must be 1/4 blood quantum Alaska Native or, in the absence of proof of blood quantum, be "regarded as" an Alaska Native by a village or community and parents must also have been "regarded as" an Alaska Native.

Since 1972, over 40 years or two generations have passed. As a portion of the Alaska Native population has married and reproduced with non-Native people, the blood quantum levels of some descendants have declined and the proportion that are less than 1/4 Alaska Native blood quantum has gradually increased. It is now the case that more Alaska Natives, including some descendants of the original Alaska Natives who were admitted as shareholders to ANCSA corporations after 1971, fall below the 1/4 blood quantum required for Alaska Natives to be eligible to hunt and utilize marine mammals. While this pattern is true of all Alaska Native coastal regions, qualitative and quantitative data indicate it is far more pronounced among southern groups occupying the Gulf of Alaska region (Chugach, Cook Inlet, Koniag, Sealaska) than in other parts of coastal Alaska. This means that it is increasingly difficult or impossible for these families to pass on their marine mammals hunting and handicraft manufacturing traditions and practices to their descendants.

This report has addressed the Marine Mammal Protection Act's regulatory definition and enforcement of Alaska Native eligibility.

Discussion was presented on the important concepts of tribes, tribal enrollment, tribes in Alaska, and blood quantum, each of which are relevant to the topic of the definition of Alaska Natives and to how the criteria defining an Alaska Native might be changed. The definition of Alaska Native both in ANCSA and in the MMPA (which was modeled on the ANCSA definition) were examined in regard to the source of the 1/4 blood quantum criteria used in both. There is additional language in both ANCSA and the MMPA regulatory definition that provides that persons who cannot prove 1/4 blood quantum are to be regarded as Alaska Natives if their parents were regarded as Alaska Natives by the community or village in which they resided. This provision was placed in ANCSA to make it possible for persons to be admitted to ANCSA corporations if they could not demonstrate 1/4 blood quantum with records. An undetermined number of persons were enrolled in ANCSA as a result of this provision. To date, neither NMFS nor USFWS have provided a means for Alaska Natives who are unable to demonstrate 1/4 blood quantum to utilize this provision to be deemed eligible to hunt and utilize marine mammals.

The recent history of Alaska Native organizations addressing the issue of the MMPA's regulatory definition and its effects was traced from 2009 until 2016. The issue was initially raised by Koniag region groups in 2009 and they forwarded a resolution to AFN for consideration. In the ensuing years, the issue was brought before various marine mammal co-management organizations for discussion. In 2011 the Indigenous Peoples Council on Marine Mammals took a position of neutrality after considerable discussion. Proponents for changing the definition recommend use of the concept of lineal descendants from ANCSA original shareholders and original tribal enrollees, while other advocates took the position that tribes should be the determiners of eligibility to hunt and utilize marine mammals if the criteria were to be changed. Agency responders to Alaska Native requests for revising the regulatory definition pointed out that there was not a unified Alaska Native position about changing the regulatory definition and took no action.

Trends in the proportion of Alaska Natives with less than 1/4 blood quantum were examined with various qualitative and numerical data. No public data are available on the current percentage of Alaska Natives of various ages who are of less than 1/4 blood quantum. Sealaska Corporation data show that as of 2001, the shareholder population, comprising original cohort and their descendants, included nearly 30% of less than 1/4 blood quantum (Table 4). BIA CDIB enrollment data from 2006-2016 show that for all Alaska Native coastal groups, the proportion of new enrollees of less than 1/4 blood quantum was 30%. The data also show that the rate of less than 1/4 blood quantum in new BIA enrollees rose about 20% over the last five years of the period.

In coastal areas, regional groups showed substantial variation in the rate of less than 1/4 blood quantum enrollees over the 2006-2016 period as well as variations in increases in the rate over the last five years of the period. Four western and northern Alaska Native coastal groups had both low rates of 1/4 blood quantum enrollment over the period (less than 20%) as well as low rates of increase (less than 2.5%) over the most recent five years. By contrast, three southern Alaska Native coastal groups had both high rates of blood quantum enrollment over the period (greater than 50%) as well as high rates of increase (greater than 10%).

Many Alaska Natives, especially from the Gulf of Alaska communities, reported major concerns about the numbers of younger people in their communities who are ineligible to hunt or utilize marine mammals. They are deeply concerned about their inability to pass on their cultural traditions and to have access to marine mammals for food in the future. They point to the basic unfairness of some descendants of the same person being eligible to utilize marine mammals while other descendants from that person are ineligible due to being below 1/4 blood quantum. Alaska Natives, some of whose descendants are criminalized for engaging in cultural traditions handed down and practiced over thousands of years, deeply resent this situation.

Some Alaska Natives raised concerns about how proposing to change the MMPA regulatory definition of Alaska Native could lead to unanticipated and detrimental outcomes. They point out that the present law provides a blanket exemption for coastal Alaska Natives and, at least for hunting, has relatively few bureaucratic requirements. They are concerned that through this process, agencies will introduce additional changes beyond merely the criterion change that could result in loss of the Alaska Native exemption, elimination of urban coastal communities, and increased agency requirements for hunting and using marine mammals.

In the course of the study, alternative criteria were identified from various sources including BIA CDIB enrollment, tribal enrollment, and lineal descendancy from original ANCSA shareholders or tribal members. In presentations to ANOs, information on the alternatives was provided through a handout (see Appendix 1). In the discussions that ensued among members of various boards, different views and positions became apparent about whether change in the regulatory definition should be sought or not and if so what an appropriate alternative(s) might be. Some proponents expressed a desire to see broadly inclusive criteria (CDIBs) while others wished to see local tribes make the determination. Table 14 summarizes primary alternative criterion, considerations about them, and how to implement them.

NMFS and USFWS officials involved in the enforcement of provisions of the MMPA reported that the 1/4 blood quantum standard is what they use to define Alaska Native status. Alaska Natives are not required to have documentation of their status with them when hunting. If a question arises, individuals may be asked to provide documentation at a later time. Taggers are not required to determine the status of a hunter when an animal is tagged and the tagging forms used to report the harvested animal do not ask for documentation demonstrating the Native status of the hunters.

A number of critical questions face Alaska Natives in addressing this issue.

Table 14 Primary Alternative for MMPA Regulatory Criteria Defining Alaska Native

Alternative Criterion	Considerations	How to implement
Reduce blood quantum (for example, 1/8)	Alaska Natives who are less than 1/8 would be ineligible; the number of Alaska Natives in this category will increase in the future	Regulation revision
Use lineal descendancy from original tribal member or original ANCSA shareholder (without blood quantum)	ANCSA amendments allow non-Native descendants; some Alaska Natives are descended from Natives who are neither original shareholders nor original tribal enrollees	Statutory amendment or Regulatory revision
Use CDIB (without blood quantum)	CDIB may not indicate tribal membership or whether person is coastal Alaska Native	Statutory amendment or Regulatory revision
Use tribal membership (criteria determined by tribes)	Tribal enrollment criteria vary. Some tribes have non-Alaska Native members; some tribes use blood quantum while others do not; could result in 200 or more determinations; some Alaska Natives are not tribal members	Statutory amendment or Regulatory revision
Use tribal membership plus tribal certification of eligibility (criteria determined by tribes)	Tribes would be required to certify Alaska Native status of members eligible for MMPA, not all Alaska Natives are members of tribes	Statutory amendment or Regulatory revision
Implement "regarded as ... Alaska Native" provision (without blood quantum)	Stipulate that Alaska Native community, village, group or organization considers the person to be Alaska Native	Statutory amendment or Regulatory Revision possibly Administrative action

1. Is there a proposed change that can be broadly accepted by all or nearly all coastal Alaska Native groups?
2. What is that proposed change?
3. Can the proposed change be accomplished without endangering the valued features of the current MMPA regime, i.e. Alaska Native exemption, Alaska Native residents of all coastal communities eligible, no licensing requirements, no reporting requirements (except for tagged animals)?
4. Through what means should the change in the definition of Alaska Native be pursued—amendment to the

statute, regulatory rule-making, or possibly another route implementing the unutilized "regarded as..." language?

There are also a number of key questions which were raised by various Alaska Natives during the research about which there currently is little or no information but which are important to consider.

1. How many Alaska Natives are currently hunting marine mammals and manufacturing handicrafts from marine mammal materials? How does that vary by region and species?
2. What has been the trend in the number of marine mammal utilizers by region and species over the past 10 or 20 years?
3. What is the present biological status of various marine mammal species?
4. If there is a change in the criteria, how many additional utilizers of marine mammals will become eligible? How many will become active in hunting and manufacturing?
5. What will the impact of additional hunters be on the biological status of various species in various regions?
6. What will the impact of additional utilizers be on Alaska Natives who currently depend on the marine mammal materials for various subsistence uses?

REFERENCES

Arnold, Robert (1976). *Alaska Native Land Claims.* Anchorage: Alaska Native Foundation.

Bassett, Neil Risser (Nov. 23, 1971) [Memo of Agreement between Bureau of Indian Affairs and Bureau of Land Management]. Neil Risser Bassett Collection, 1940-1991. The University of Alaska Anchorage Archives and Special Collections Department (Series 4, Folder 1), University of Alaska, Anchorage, Alaska.

Black, Lydia (2004). *Russians in Alaska: 1732-1867*, University of Alaska Press. Fairbanks, Alaska.

Daniel, Carol (2011). Marine Mammal Protection Act regulatory definition of "Alaska Native." Memorandum submitted to Julie Kitka, President of AFN. May 11.

Department of the Interior, Bureau of Indian Affairs (1995). "Indian Entities Recognized and Eligible To Receive Services From The United States Bureau of Indian Affairs." *Federal Register* 60:(32) Thursday, February 16, 1995.

Edmo, Se-ah-dom (2016). "The Problems of Modern Indian Identity: Intersectionality, the American Dream, the Myth of Scarcity, Disenrollment, and Belonging." IN Edmo, S, Young, J. and Parker, A. (eds) *American Indian Identity: Citizenship, Membership and Blood.* Santa Barbara and Denver: Praeger.

Emmons, George (1990). *The Tlingit Indians.* Seattle: University of Washington Press.

ESG (1985). *The 1985 ANCSA Study* (Draft). Washington, DC: US Department of the Interior.

Fall, James (2016). "Regional Patterns of Fish and Wildlife Harvests in Contemporary Alaska." *Arctic 69* (1): 47-64.

Federal Field Commission for Development and Planning in Alaska (1968). "Alaska Natives and the Land" (October 1968). Washington, DC: US Department of the Interior.

Garroute, Eva (2001). "The Racial Formation of American Indians: Negotiating Legitimate Identities within Tribal and Federal Law." *American Indian Quarterly* 25 (2):224-239.

Gover, Kirsty (2008/2009). "Genealogy as Continuity: Explaining the Growing Tribal Preference for Descent Rules in Membership Governance in the United States." *American Indian Law Review* 33(1): 243-309.

Hamilton, Lawrence, Saito, Kei; Loring, Philip; Lammers, Richard, and Huntington, Henry (2016). "Climigration? Population and climate change in Arctic Alaska." *Population and Environment: 1-19.* DOI 10.1007/s11111-016-0259-6.

Jackson, Sheldon (1880). *Alaska, and Missions on the North Pacific Coast.* New York: Dodd, Mead & Company.

Langdon, Steve (1989). "Prospects for Co-Management under the Marine Mammal Protection Act in Alaska." IN Pinkerton L. (ed.) *Co-Management of Fisheries.* Vancouver, B.C.: University of British Columbia Press.

Langdon, Steve (2013). "Unreciprocated 'Reverence': 'Papers', Political Recognition, and Tlingit Engagement with US Governmentality in the Late Nineteenth Century." *Ethnohistory* 60(3):505-536.

Langdon, Steve (2014). *The Native People of Alaska: Traditional Living in a Northern Land.* Anchorage, Alaska: Greatland Press.

Marszalek, John (2004). *Commander of All Lincoln's Armies: A Life of General Henry W. Halleck*. Cambridge, Mass: Belknap Press.

O'Brien, Sharon (1991). "Tribes and Indians: With Whom Does the United States Maintain a Relationship?" *Notre Dame Law Review* 66: 1481.

Parker, Alan (2016a). "Indian Identity and the Role of the Tribal Governments Today." IN Edmo S., Young J. and Parker A. (eds) *American Indian Identity: Citizenship, Membership and Blood.* Santa Barbara and Denver: Praeger.

Parker, Alan (2016b). "Replace the Paradigm of Tribal Membership with the Paradigm of Tribal Citizenship." IN Edmo, S., Young, J. and Parker, A. (eds) *American Indian Identity: Citizenship, Membership and Blood.* Santa Barbara and Denver: Praeger.

Robertson, Dwanna L. 2013. "A Necessary Evil: Framing an American Indian Legal Identity." *American Indian Culture and Research Journal* 37:4.

Samuels, Ellen (2014). *Fantasies of Identification: Disability, Gender, Race.* New York: NYU Press.

Schmidt, Ryan (2011). "American Indian Identity and Blood Quantum in the 21st Century: A Critical Review." *Journal of Anthropology,* Vol. 2011: 1-9

Spruhan, Paul (2006). "A Legal History of Blood Quantum in Federal Indian Law to 1935." *South Dakota Law Review* 51: 1-50.

Thornton, Russell (1997). "Tribal membership requirements and the demography of 'old' and 'new' Native Americans." *Population Research and Policy Review* 16 (1): 33–42.

US Bureau of Indian Affairs (1993). "Indian Entities Recognized and Eligible to Receive Services from the United States Bureau of Indian Affairs." *Federal Register* 58: 54364–54369.

Voorhees, Hannah (2015). "Subsistence Biologies: 'Blood Quantum'-Based Alaska Native Hunting Rights in a Climate of Scarcity." Paper delivered in the session *Governing Indigeneity: Bureaucracy, Vulnerability, and the State in the Americans* at the annual meeting of the American Anthropological Association held in Denver.

Young, Jessie (2016). "Tribal Citizenship and Indian Identity." IN Edmo, S, Young, J. and Parker, A. (eds) *American Indian Identity: Citizenship, Membership and Blood.* Santa Barbara and Denver: Praeger.

APPENDIX 1: INFORMATIONAL HANDOUT PROVIDED AT MMPA PRESENTATIONS

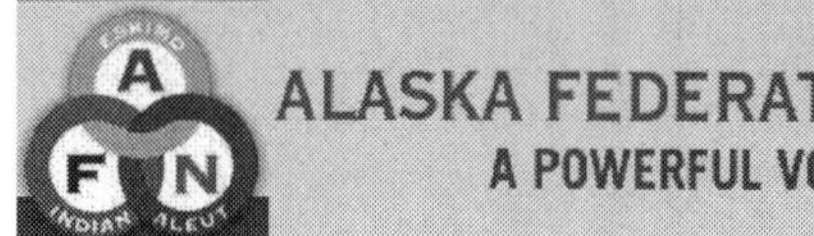

Alaska Native Determination under the Marine Mammal Protection Act (MMPA)

Information for Research Project on Eligibility Criteria

Dr. Steve J. Langdon, Ph.D.

Background – In response to an AFN convention resolution to change the regulatory ¼ blood requirement under MMPA, AFN began working with the Indigenous People's Council for Marine Mammals, a coalition of marine mammal Native organizations, to determine Alaska Native views on the issue. AFN and IPCoMM agreed to initiate a study of the issues surrounding the ¼ blood requirement and possible alternative eligibility criteria. Dr. Steve J. Langdon, Ph.D. was contracted by the Sealaska Heritage Institute to conduct the research. The research project will not initiate any action to change the current regulations. The purpose of this document is to present information for discussion and advisory views by Alaska Native organizations on key questions. The first page presents the current definition and possible alternatives. The second page consists of questions for discussion by Alaska Native organizations and tribes about the issue.

Currently there are three ways MMPA regulations define Alaska Natives. A blood quantum of ¼ is required in two of them. The other states that in the absence of evidence of blood quantum, other means can used to demonstrate who is "regarded as" a Native by their community. Options to consider include 1) no change and 2) change – with several alternatives, and perhaps more, to consider.

1. <u>Do Not Change the regulations</u> – criteria for Alaska Native determination would remain one-fourth degree or more of Alaska Indian, Eskimo or Aleut blood, or combination thereof. Maintain case by case determination of eligibility based on village status for Alaska Natives of less than one-quarter blood quantum.

2 A. <u>Change blood quantum to 1/8</u> – insert 1/8 in the definition of Alaska Native as an <u>alternative</u>.

COMMENT: This would continue the use of blood quantum and meet almost all current issues of eligibility.

2 B. <u>Tribal enrollment</u> – specify tribal enrollment as an <u>alternative.</u> Tribes as sovereign governments determine their own criteria for membership (enrollment).

COMMENT: If a person is enrolled in an Alaska Native tribe and has Alaska Native ancestry as determined by the tribe, then they would qualify. Not all Alaska Natives are members of tribes. NOTE: Some tribes enroll Native Americans who are not Alaska Natives as members. Such tribal members would not be eligible under MMPA.

2 C. <u>BIA enrollment</u> – specify BIA enrollment as an <u>alternative.</u> BIA enrollment requires a Certificate of Determination of Indian Blood (CDIB) and issuance of a card.

COMMENT: Someone enrolled by the BIA with a CDIB is eligible for BIA services, no matter the blood quantum. BIA enrollment specifies only Alaska Native status – as such it could be an alternative.

2 D. Lineal descendant – specify lineal descent from original tribal enrollee or original Alaska Native corporation shareholder as criteria with no blood quantum required as an alternative.

COMMENT: This criteria would avoid blood quantum and insure that a person was of Alaska Native descent. There may be some Alaska Natives who would not qualify.

2 E. Other possibilities – regional Alaska Native determination of eligibility by tribal commissions, for example Aleut Marine Mammal Commission and Bristol Bay Marine Mammal Commission.

3. Questions to consider:

We hope that every tribal government or Native organization involved with marine mammal issues will take the time to address each of the following questions. It is crucial that all interested tribes participate in determining how to address this issue. We thank you sincerely for your time.

A. Is the MMPA regulation setting the one-quarter blood quantum criterion for determination of Alaska Native eligibility ~~as~~ a concern to the organization/tribe?

B. Does the organization/tribe anticipate descendants not qualifying under the one-quarter quantum criteria in the near future?

C. Does the organization/tribe wish to retain the one-quarter criterion?

D. If the organization/tribe would like to see the one-quarter criterion changed, which of the following is preferred?

- Tribal Enrollment
- BIA Enrollment
- Lineal Descent (original tribal or ANCSA corporation member)

E. Are there other alternative criteria, not listed above, that would be preferred by the organization/tribe? Is so, what are they?

F. Should Alaska Natives begin a process seeking to amend the MMPA Alaska Native determination criteria currently found in the regulations?

PLEASE RATE FROM 1 – 5

1 – Not important or don't change

2 – Small important – other matters more important

3 – Medium important – monitor but don't take action

4 – Very important, continue to discussion to arrive at shared position

5 – Extremely important, act immediately

APPENDIX 2: MEETINGS OF ANOS WHERE PRESENTATIONS WERE GIVEN

Organization	Date	Location
Chugach Regional Resources Commission	Oct. 8, 2015	Anchorage
Alaska Beluga Whale Council	Nov. 10, 2015	Anchorage
Aleut Marine Mammal Commission	Nov. 13, 2015	Anchorage
Indigenous People's Commission on Marine Mammals	Dec. 3, 2015	Anchorage
Hydaburg Cooperative Association	Dec. 10, 2015	Teleconference
Klawock Cooperative Association	Dec. 11, 2015	Klawock
POW- Tribal Sea Otter Commission	Dec. 12, 2015	Klawock
Sitka Marine Mammal Commission	Jan. 19, 2016	Sitka
Organized Village of Saxman	Jan. 20, 2016	Saxman
Ketchikan Indian Corporation	Jan. 21, 2016	Ketchikan
Central Council of Tlingit and Haida Indians	Jan. 28, 2016	Juneau
Douglas Indian Association	Feb. 2, 2016	Teleconference
Inupiat Community of the Arctic Slope (ICAS)	March 4, 2016	Barrow
Chugach Rural Resources Commission	March 15, 2016	Anchorage
Kodiak Roundtable	April 8, 2016	Kodiak
Alaska Sea Otter and Sea Lion Commission	April 18, 2016	Anchorage
Hoonah Indian Association	April 27, 2016	Hoonah
Alaska Harbor Seal Commission	April 28, 2016	Juneau
Organized Village of Kake	July 21, 2016	Teleconference

APPENDIX 3: INTERVIEWS CONCERNING MMPA ALASKA NATIVE ELIGIBILITY CRITERIA

Federal Agency Personnel	Organization	Position
Jon Kurland	NMFS	Director, Protected Resources
Alisha Falstad	NMFS	Enforcement Attorney
Ron Antaya	NMFS	Enforcement Agent
Charles Hamilton	FWS	Management
Crystal Leonetti	FWS	Native Liasion
Brad Benter	FWS	Tagging Program Director
Rory Stark	FWS	Enforcement
Ken Lord	FWS	US Attorney's Office
John Boone	FWS Contractor, Valdez	Tagger
Jon Rowan	FWS Contractor, Klawock	Tagger
Jolene John	BIA	Tribal Operations Officer
Other Interviewees	**Affiliation**	**Position**
Tim Andrew	AVCP	Director of Natural Resources
Edgar Blatchford	Chugach Alaska	Former Board Member
Carol Daniels	Alaska Federation of Natives	Attorney/Former AFN Employee
Perry Eaton	Koniag	Former Board Member
James Fall	Alaska Department of Fish and Game, Subsistence Division	Research Director
Jana Harcharek	North Slope Borough	Cultural and History Program Director
Taqulik Hepa	North Slope Borough	Director of Wildlife Management
Robert Henrichs	Eyak Village	Council Member
Carl Jack	US Fish and Wildlife Service	Retired
Fred Kavlik	Bering Sea Elders	Coordinator
Harold Martin	TASSC	Former Member
Gordon Pullar	KANA	Former Executive Director
Sky Starkey	Alaska Migratory Bird Co-Management Council	Attorney
Mike Williams	Akiak	Tribal Member/Yup'ik Leader
Alaska Native Marine Mammal Co-Management Organization Personnel	**Affiliation**	**Position**
Helen Adermann	Bristol Bay Native Association	Marine Mammal Coordinator
Harry K Brower	Alaska Eskimo Whaling Commission	Chairman
Willie Goodwin	Alaska Beluga Whale Council	Chairman
Patrick Kosbruk	Bristol Bay Marine Mammal Commission	Member
Mike Miller	Sitka Marine Mammal Commission	Chairman
Patrick Norman	Chugach Rural Resources Commission	Member
Patty Schwalenberg	Chugach Regional Resources Commission	Executive Director
Margaret Roberts	Alaska Sea Otter and Sea Lion Commission	Chair
Vera Metcalfe	Eskimo Walrus Commission	Executive Director
Hub Tribal Personnel	**Affiliation**	**Position**
Gene Peltola, Sr.	Orutsararmuit Native Council (Bethel tribe)	Executive Director
Emma Pate	Nome Eskimo Community	Executive Director
Jacob Martin	Nome Eskimo Community	Subsistence Specialist
Kerin Kramer	Eyak (Cordova)	Executive Director
Dorothy Larson	Quryung (Dillingham)	Executive Director
JJ Marsh	Sun'aq (Kodiak)	Executive Director
Thomas Olemaun	Native Village of Barrow	Executive Director
Brenda Stoopes	Native Village of Kotzebue	Executive Director
Cyrus Harris	Native Village of Kotzebue	Council Member

APPENDIX 4: AFN RESOLUTION 09-08

ALASKA FEDERATION OF NATIVES, INC.

2009 ANNUAL CONVENTION

RESOLUTION 09-08

TITLE: SUPPORTING REGULATORY CHANGES TO ALLOW TRIBAL MEMBERS AND/OR ALASKA NATIVE ANCSA DESCENDENTS TO TAKE, POSSESS AND UTILIZE SEA OTTERS FOR SUBSISTENCE AND HANDICRAFT

WHEREAS: The indigenous people of Alaska have harvested sea otters since time immemorial for many uses that include regalia, clothing, art, and trade; and

WHEREAS: The Marine Mammal Protection Act was made law in 1972 and states that only coastal Indians, Aleuts and Eskimos are able to take marine mammals for subsistence or handicraft purposes; and

WHEREAS: The Code of Federal Regulations (CFR) implementing the Marine Mammal Protection Act of 1972 uses the original definition of "Native" established in the Alaska Native Claims Settlement Act (ANCSA) of 1971; and

WHEREAS: In the CFRs, "Native" means a citizen of the United States who is a person of one-fourth degree or more Alaska Indian (including Tsimshian Indians not enrolled in the Metlakatla Indian Community) Eskimo, or Aleut blood, or combination thereof, or originally enrolled under Section 5 of ANCSA; and

WHEREAS: These regulations have divided Alaskan Natives into two categories of "Natives" and "Descendants of"; and

WHEREAS: Hunting, proper hide preparation and skin sewing are traditional activities that are essential components of one's cultural identify, and these skills are taught and passed from one generation to the next; and

WHEREAS: Sea otter hunting, hide preparation and skin sewing are important in the Alutiiq culture; and

WHEREAS: The current regulations prohibit teaching and mentoring our youth on the skill and knowledge of sea otter hunting and handicraft if they are below ¼ blood quantum, negatively impacting the Alutiiq and the other Alaska Native cultures; and

NOW THEREFORE BE IT RESOLVED that the CFR (50 CFR 18) be revised, if required, to allow each Alaska Native Tribe to authorize and allow Alaska Native ANCSA Descendants to non-wastefully take, possess and utilize sea otters for subsistence or handicraft purposes; and

BE IT FURTHER RESOLVED that the regulations be further amended to allow Alaska Native members of Alaska Native tribal governments to non-wastefully take, possess and utilize sea otters for subsistence and handicraft purposes; and

29

BE IT FURTHER RESOLVED that the Department of Interior and appropriate agencies take the necessary steps to implement this resolution immediately.

SUBMITTED BY: KONIAG REGION

COMMITTEE ACTION: DO PASS

CONVENTION ACTION: AMENDED AND PASSED

APPENDIX 5: AFN RESOLUTION 10-11

ALASKA FEDERATION OF NATIVES, INC.

2010 AFN CONVENTION

RESOLUTION 10-11

TITLE: THE PROTECTION AND CONTINUATION OF CUSTOMARY AND TRADITIONAL PRACTICES FOR MARINE MAMMAL SUBSISTENCE FOR FUTURE GENERATIONS

WHEREAS: Alaska Native peoples have developed rich cultures and practices around marine mammal harvest and utilization since time immemorial, and these practices continue today; and

WHEREAS: Hunting, proper hide preparation and skin sewing are customary and traditional activities that are essential components of one's cultural identity, and these skills are taught and passed from one generation to the next; and

WHEREAS: The Marine Mammal Protection Act was made law in 1972 prohibiting the take, import and export of marine mammals by United States citizens; and

WHEREAS: Section ID1(b) was included in the Marine Mammal Protection Act to exempt coastal Indians, Aleuts and Eskimos from these take prohibitions for non-wasteful subsistence and handicraft purposes; and

WHEREAS: The Code of Federal Regulations (CFR) implementing the Marine Mammal Protection Act of 1972 uses the original definition of "Native" as established in the Alaska Native Claims Settlement Act (ANCSA) of 1971; and

WHEREAS: In the CFRs, "Native" means a citizen of the United States who is a person of one-fourth degree or more Alaska Indian (including Tsimshian Indians enrolled or not enrolled in the Metlakatla Indian Community) Eskimo, or Aleut blood, or combination thereof, or originally enrolled under Section 5 of ANCSA; and

WHEREAS: The regulations are more restrictive than the language in the Marine Mammal Protection Act and inconsistent with the legislative history; and

WHEREAS: Families today are being affected by these regulations as some children or grandchildren do not meet this minimum blood quantum; and

WHEREAS: Marine mammal hunting, utilization and handicraft remain vital to the cultural identity and survival of Alaska Native cultures and their economic well being; and

WHEREAS: Cultural traditions and knowledge are in danger of being lost because of these regulations; and

28

WHEREAS: In 2009, the delegates to the Alaska Federation of Natives passed resolution 09-08 urging the Secretary of Interior take immediate and all necessary action to ensure that lineal descendants and Alaska Native tribal members of less than one-fourth blood quantum may continue their subsistence traditions pertaining to sea otter harvest and use; and

WHEREAS: The regulations remain unchanged, requiring that an Alaska Native individual be of one-fourth or more Alaska Native blood quantum or originally enrolled under ANCSA in order to participate in sea otter or other marine mammal subsistence activities; and

NOW THEREFORE BE IT RESOLVED by the Delegates to the 2010 Annual Convention of the Alaska Federation of Natives Inc., that the Alaska Federation of Natives petition the Secretaries of Interior and Commerce to change the definition of "Alaskan Native" under 50 CFR 18.3 and 50 CFR 216.3 to include lineal Alaska Natives descendants of less than one-fourth blood quantum.

SUBMITTED BY: KONIAG REGION

COMMITTEE ACTION: DO PASS

CONVENTION ACTION: REFER TO AFN BOARD SUBSISTENCE COMMITTEE

APPENDIX 6: NCAI RESOLUTION 2010-015

NCAI HEADQUARTERS
1516 P Street, N.W.
Washington, DC 20005
202.466.7767
202.466.7797 fax
www.ncai.org

NATIONAL CONGRESS OF AMERICAN INDIANS

The National Congress of American Indians
Resolution #ABQ-10-015

TITLE: The Protection and Continuation of Customary and Traditional Practices for Marine Mammal Subsistence for Future Generations

WHEREAS, we, the members of the National Congress of American Indians of the United States, invoking the divine blessing of the Creator upon our efforts and purposes, in order to preserve for ourselves and our descendants the inherent sovereign rights of our Indian nations, rights secured under Indian treaties and agreements with the United States, and all other rights and benefits to which we are entitled under the laws and Constitution of the United States, to enlighten the public toward a better understanding of the Indian people, to preserve Indian cultural values, and otherwise promote the health, safety and welfare of the Indian people, do hereby establish and submit the following resolution; and

WHEREAS, the National Congress of American Indians (NCAI) was established in 1944 and is the oldest and largest national organization of American Indian and Alaska Native tribal governments; and

WHEREAS, Alaska Native peoples have developed rich cultures and practices around marine mammal harvest and utilization since time immemorial, and these practices continue today; and

WHEREAS, hunting, proper hide preparation and skin sewing are customary and traditional activities that are essential components of one's cultural identity, and these skills are taught and passed from one generation to the next; and

WHEREAS, the Marine Mammal Protection Act was made law in 1972 prohibiting the take, import and export of marine mammals by United States citizens; and

WHEREAS, Section 101(b) was included in the Marine Mammal Protection Act to exempt coastal Indians, Aleuts and Eskimos from these take prohibitions for non-wasteful subsistence and handicraft purposes; and

WHEREAS, the Code of Federal Regulations (CFR) implementing the Marine Mammal Protection Act of 1972 uses the original definition of "Native" as established in the Alaska Native Claims Settlement Act (ANCSA) of 1971; and

WHEREAS, in the CFRs, "Native" means a citizen of the United States who is a person of one-fourth degree or more Alaska Indian (including Tsimshian Indians enrolled or not enrolled in the Metlakatla Indian Community) Eskimo, or Aleut blood, or combination thereof, or originally enrolled under Section 5 of ANCSA; and

WHEREAS, the regulations are more restrictive than the language in the Marine Mammal Protection Act and inconsistent with the legislative history; and

WHEREAS, families today are being affected by these regulations as some children or grandchildren do not meet this minimum blood quantum; and

WHEREAS, marine mammal hunting, utilization and handicraft remain vital to the cultural identity and survival of Alaska Native cultures and their economic well being; and

WHEREAS, cultural traditions and knowledge are in danger of being lost because of these regulations; and

WHEREAS, in 2009, the delegates to the Alaska Federation of Natives passed resolution 09-08 urging the Secretary of Interior take immediate and all necessary action to ensure that lineal descendants and Alaska Native tribal members of less that ¼ blood quantum may continue their subsistence traditions pertaining to sea otter harvest and use; and

WHEREAS, the regulations remain unchanged, requiring that an Alaska Native individual be of one-fourth or more Alaska Native blood quantum or originally enrolled under ANCSA in order to participate in sea otter or other marine mammal subsistence activities.

NOW THEREFORE BE IT RESOLVED, that the NCAI fully support and advocate for the petition to the Secretaries of Interior and Commerce to change the definition of "Alaskan Native" under 50 CFR 18.3 and 50 CFR 216.3 to include lineal Alaska Natives descendants of less than one-fourth blood quantum, those originally enrolled in the Alaska Native Claims Settlement Act, and Alaska Natives enrolled in a federally recognized tribal government; and

BE IT FURTHER RESOLVED, that this resolution shall be the policy of NCAI until it is withdrawn or modified by subsequent resolution.

CERTIFICATION

The foregoing resolution was adopted by the General Assembly at the 2010 Annual Convention of the National Congress of American Indians, held at the Albuquerque Convention Center in Albuquerque, NM on November 14-19, 2010, with a quorum present.

President

ATTEST:

Recording Secretary

APPENDIX 7: SEA OTTER AND SEA LION COMMISSION WHITE PAPER

MMPA REGULATIONS AND THE DEFINITION OF ALASKA NATIVE
February 3, 2010

The Marine Mammal Protection Act was passed in 1972. It created a general moratorium on marine mammal takes, with certain exceptions. This includes Section 101(b), which exempts "*any Indian, Aleut or Eskimo that dwells on the coast of the North Pacific Ocean or the Arctic Ocean*" from the general take prohibitions to allow for subsistence and handicraft purposes, provided that the takes are not wasteful, and that handicrafts are not mass produced.

The act conferred management authority for marine mammals to the Department of Interior and the Department of Commerce. The Department of Interior and Commerce put forth regulations interpreting the Act (50 CFR 18.3 and 50 CFR 216.3 respectively).

The regulations read:

> "*Alaskan Native means a person defined in the Alaska Native Claims Settlement Act (43 U.S.C. section 1603(b) (85 Stat.588)) as a citizen of the United States who is one-fourth degree or more Alaska Indian (including Tsimshian Indians enrolled or not enrolled in the Metlakatla Indian Community), Eskimo, or Aleut blood, or combination thereof. The term also includes any Native, either or both of whose adoptive parents are not Native….Any citizen enrolled by the Secretary pursuant to section 5 of the Alaska Native Claims Settlement Act shall be conclusively presumed to be an Alaskan Native for purposes of this part.*"

The regulations stipulate ¼ blood quantum, whereas the Act stipulates a coastal Alaska Native.

This inconsistency between the regulations and the statute is an issue that is affecting our communities today and will become an increasing problem into the future. In our communities, there are children who do not meet the minimum blood quantum, yet their parents, grandparents and other family members continue their traditional and customary practices including marine mammal hunting and sewing. This is harming our communities. Our traditions are in danger of being lost, or our members are made to feel like criminals and fear prosecution for teaching their kids.

In September 2009, the Kodiak Island Roundtable passed the resolution entitled "*Supporting regulatory changes to allow Tribal Members and/or Alaska Native ANCSA descendants to take, possess, and utilize sea otters for subsistence and handicraft.*" This resolution was forwarded to the Alaska Federation of Natives (AFN) and resolution 09-08 was passed by the full AFN Convention on October 24, 2009.

Other statutes and regulations have different definitions of Alaska Native. The Indian Health Service definition stipulates that a person be of Indian descent and is a member of their Indian community. The Silverhand program administered by the State of Alaska, which identifies authentic Alaska Native art in the marketplace, has recently changed their eligibility requirement; the blood quantum requirement was replaced with a requirement than an individual be a member of an Alaska Native tribe (and Alaska Native).

We firmly believe that it our sovereign right as federally recognized tribes to determine our membership. We believe that those born into the tribe have the same right to harvest all the resources we depend upon.

The regulations **NEED** to be changed to allow for Alaska tribal members of Alaska Native blood and lineal descendants.

APPENDIX 8: FWS AND NMFS LETTER TO IPCOMM 2014

NOAA
FISHERIES

October 3, 2014

Mike Miller, Chair
Indigenous People's Council on Marine Mammals
800 E. Dimond Blvd., Suite 3-615
Anchorage, Alaska 99515

Maude Blair, Vice President
Alaska Federation of Natives
1577 C Street, Suite 300
Anchorage, AK 99501

Dear Mr. Miller and Ms. Blair:

The U.S. Fish and Wildlife Service (FWS) and the National Marine Fisheries Service (NMFS) jointly implement the Marine Mammal Protection Act and the Endangered Species Act. Under both of these Acts, coastal dwelling Alaska Native peoples retain their rights to hunt marine mammals for subsistence purposes. The two agencies have nearly identical regulatory definitions of "Alaska Native" under the MMPA. The FWS definition can be found at 50 CFR Section 18.3 and the NMFS definition is at 50 CFR Section 216.3. Both definitions are enclosed for reference.

The FWS has been contacted by several Tribal Governments, expressing concern that the current regulatory definition may be too limiting to Tribes and their members. The FWS and NMFS recognize that both the Indigenous People's Council on Marine Mammals (IPCoMM) and the Alaska Federation of Natives (AFN) have vested interest in subsistence related regulatory definitions. As such we request that IPCoMM and AFN's Subsistence Committee review the current regulatory definitions and advise FWS and NMFS as to whether your respective organizations believe a change is needed. If a change is warranted, please identify in your comments what should be addressed, and if you desire, propose specific language you would like us to consider. Any change could affect the way subsistence harvests are conducted and managed, so if you do support consideration of a change, we would be interested in your thoughts as to how best to proceed so that all affected stakeholders can participate in that process.

The FWS and NMFS have enjoyed a longstanding co-management relationship with Tribes and Alaska Native Organizations. We look forward to hearing your input on the current regulatory definitions and engaging further if your organizations believe that change is warranted. Please contact either agency with questions and copy both agencies with any written responses, including: Crystal Leonetti (FWS) at 907-786-3868; Timothy Jennings (FWS) at 907-786-3505; and Jon Kurland (NMFS) at 907-586-7638.

Sincerely,

Timothy Jennings
Assistant Regional Director, Region 7
Fisheries and Ecological Services
U.S. Fish and Wildlife Service

Jonathan M. Kurland
Assistant Regional Administrator
for Protected Resources
NOAA Fisheries, Alaska Region

Enclosure

APPENDIX 9: TLINGIT AND HAIDA RESOLUTION 16-19 2016

CENTRAL COUNCIL
Tlingit and Haida Indian Tribes of Alaska
Edward K. Thomas Building
9097 Glacier Highway • Juneau, Alaska 99801

CENTRAL COUNCIL OF TLINGIT AND HAIDA INDIAN TRIBES OF ALASKA
Eighty-First Annual Tribal Assembly
April 20-22, 2016
Juneau, Alaska

Resolution TA/ 16-19

Title: In Support of Changing the Definition of Blood Quantum in the Marine Mammal Regulations to Descendancy

By: Kasaan Tlingit and Haida Community Council

WHEREAS, the Central Council of Tlingit and Haida Indian tribes of Alaska (Central Council) is a federally recognized tribe with more than 30,000 tribal citizens; and

WHEREAS, Central Council does not support the U.S. Fish and Wildlife's and National Marine Fisheries Service regulatory definition of Alaska Native as it applies to the Marine Mammal Protection Act and it's requirement of "blood quantum" in the regulations; and

WHEREAS, Central Council feels the U.S. Fish and Wildlife Service should abide by definitions within the Marine Mammal Protection Act of 1972, which states, "an Alaskan Native means a person defined in the Alaska Native Claims Settlement Act (ANCSA) as a citizen of the United States who is of one-fourth degree or more Alaska Indian (including Tsimshian Indians enrolled or not enrolled in the Metlakatla Indian Community), Eskimo, or Aleut blood or combination thereof. The term includes any native, as so defined, either or both of whose adoptive parents are not natives. It also includes in the absence of minimum blood quantum, any citizen of the United States who is regarded as an Alaskan Native by the native village or group, of which he claims to be a member, and whose father or mother is (or, if deceased, was) regarded as native by any native village or native group. Any such citizen enrolled by the Secretary of the Interior pursuant to section 5 of ANCSA shall be conclusively presumed to be an Alaska Native for purposes of this part"; and

WHEREAS, the term "native village or town" means any community, association, tribe, Band, clan or group.

NOW THEREFORE BE IT RESOLVED, that the Eighty-First Tribal Assembly of Central Council of Tlingit and Haida Indian Tribes of Alaska Delegation convened in Juneau, Alaska on April 20-22, 2016, hereby requests the removal of "blood quantum" in the definition for hunting marine mammals and request this definition be changed to recognize descendancy that could be proven by tribal enrollment cards, BIA Blood Quantum Certificates or other proof of descendancy.

Toll Free: 800.344.1432 www.ccthita.org Direct: 907.586.1432

TA Resolution 16-19 Page 2

ADOPTED this 22nd day of April 2016, by the Eighty-First Tribal Assembly of Central Council of Tlingit and Haida Indian Tribes of Alaska.

CERTIFY

President Richard J. Peterson

ATTEST

Tribal Secretary Ralph Wolfe

APPENDIX 10: ASRC PROPOSALS FOR ALASKA NATIVE DEFINITIONS IN MMPA MARCH 2016

Anchorage Office • 3900 C Street, Suite 801 • Anchorage, Alaska 99503-5963 • 907.339.6000 • FAX 907.339.6028 • 1.800.770.2772

The Alaska Native Access Card Act

Options for Including a Definition of the Term "Alaska Native" in an Amendment to the Marine Mammal Protection Act

On March 17, 2016, Senator Dan Sullivan introduced S. 2728, the "Alaska Native Access Card Act." The purpose of the bill is to facilitate the import of marine mammal products into the United States by Alaska Natives.

The Alaska Native Access Card Act proposes to amend the Marine Mammal Protection Act (MMPA), and would include within the MMPA a definition of the term "Alaska Native." As introduced, the Alaska Native Access Card Act uses a definition of the term "Alaska Native" that parallels the definition of "Alaskan Native" currently used in MMPA regulations.

This short memo sets forth alternative options for including language within the Alaska Native Access Card Act that would define the term "Alaska Native" under the MMPA.

<u>Background</u>

The MMPA allows Alaska Native individuals to take marine mammals for subsistence purposes or for creating and selling authentic native articles of handicrafts and clothing. However, the MMPA restricts the ability of Alaska Natives to import marine mammal products from other indigenous communities. Specifically, such importation can only occur through a "cultural exchange" with a "Native inhabitant of Russia, Canada, or Greenland." The MMPA defines "cultural exchange" to mean "the sharing or exchange of ideas, information, gifts, clothing, or handicrafts . . . including rendering of raw marine mammal parts as part of such exchange into clothing or handicrafts through carving, painting, sewing, or decorating."

The Alaska Native Access Card Act would address this issue by explicitly allowing Alaska Native individuals to purchase or otherwise acquire, export and re-import marine mammal products into the United States.

<u>Summary of Introduced Bill</u>

The Alaska Native Access Card Act would revise MMPA Section 101(a)(6)(A) to add a provision authorizing the importation of marine mammal products for noncommercial purposes by an Alaska Native individual presenting an Alaska Native Access Card.

Corporate Headquarters • PO Box 129 • Barrow, Alaska 99723-0129 • 907.852.8533 or 907.852.8633 • FAX 907.852.5733

The bill would also add a subsection directing the establishment of the Alaska Native Access Card. Specifically, within 90 days of the enactment of the bill, the Secretary of Commerce would be required to develop and implement a process for issuing an Access Card to any Alaska Native who applies. The Access Card would authorize the import, export and re-import of marine mammal products by Alaska Natives. The bill would require the Secretary to issue an Access Card within 30 days of receiving an application.

Finally, the bill would include a definition of the term "Alaska Native" and standardize the use of that term and similar terms throughout the MMPA. While the MMPA regulations currently define the term "Alaskan Native," the MMPA statutory text uses multiple, inconsistent terms to refer to Alaska's indigenous people (i.e., "Indian, Aleut, or Eskimo;" "Indian, Eskimo, or Aleut;" "Alaskan Native;" "Alaskan native;" "Alaska native;" and "native").

As introduced, the Alaska Native Access Card Act incorporates a definition of "Alaska Native" that similar to the definition of "Native" from Section 3 of the Alaska Native Claims Settlement Act (ANCSA); the ANCSA definition was altered to ensure the definition is inclusive of all Alaska Native individuals of Tsimshian descent. The definition also roughly parallels the definition of "Alaska Native" under MMPA regulations, at 50 C.F.R. § 216.3.

Since the introduction of the legislation, some Alaska Native groups have raised questions or concerns about the definition of "Alaska Native", specifically the blood quantum requirement. In an effort to address those concerns, ASRC has laid out five alternatives for consideration. The first three options aim to address the blood quantum concerns raised. The final two maintain a status quo approach in some fashion.

Options for Including a Definition of the Term "Alaska Native"

(1) Amend the MMPA to Define of the Term "Alaska Native" in a Manner that Includes "Descendants"

One option for defining the term "Alaska Native" under the MMPA would be to include the phrase "any Descendant of a Native" within the definition of "Alaska Native." The term "Descendant of a Native" is defined separately in ANCSA, as amended, at 43 U.S.C. § 1602(r) as follows:

> "'Descendant of a Native' means
> (1) a lineal descendant of a Native or of an individual who would have been a Native if such individual were alive on December 18, 1971, or
> (2) an adoptee of a Native or of a descendant of a Native, whose adoption
> (A) occurred prior to his or her majority, and

(B) is recognized at law or in equity;"

Thus, the expanded definition of "Alaskan Native" under the MMPA could read: "The term 'Alaskan Native' means a 'Native' or a 'Descendant of a Native' as those terms are defined in section 3 of the Alaska Native Claims Settlement Act (43 U.S.C. 1602) including Tsimshian Indians enrolled or not enrolled in the Metlakatla Indian Community."

Under this option, the bill would apply the use of the term "Alaska Native," with its expanded meaning, to all of the MMPA.

(2) Amend the MMPA to Define as Separate Terms, "Alaska Native" and "Descendant of a Native," and Utilize the Terms as Appropriate Throughout the MMPA

Alternatively, the MMPA could be amended to include separate definitions of the terms "Alaska Native" and "Descendant of a Native." This would allow the terms to be used together or independently throughout the MMPA.

By defining the two terms, the Alaska Native Access Card Act could, for example, extend the new statutory right to import marine mammal products to any Alaska Native and to any Descendant of a Native, while retaining the status quo for other provisions of the MMPA, which currently apply more narrowly to "Alaskan Natives" as defined in MMPA regulations.

(3) Eliminate Use of Definitions that Depend Upon a "Blood Quantum" Threshold, and Define the Term "Alaska Native" by Reference to Membership in an "Indian Tribe" as Defined by the Indian Self Determination and Education Assistance Act

The MMPA could be amended to include a definition of "Alaska Native" by reference to membership in an Indian tribe. A commonly used definition of "Indian tribe," at Section 4(e) of the Indian Self-Determination and Education Assistance Act, 25 U.S.C. § 450b(e) reads:

> "'Indian tribe' means any Indian tribe, band, nation, or other organized group or community, including any Alaska Native village or regional or village corporation as defined in or established pursuant to the Alaska Native Claims Settlement Act (85 Stat. 688) [43 U.S.C. 1601 et seq.], which is recognized as eligible for the special programs and services provided by the United States to Indians because of their status as Indians;"

This definition of "Indian tribe" has long been interpreted to include both Alaska Native tribes and Alaska Native corporations.[1] By defining the term "Alaska Native" by reference to membership in an Indian tribe, the dependence of that term on any "blood quantum" threshold is eliminated.

(4) Amend the MMPA to Define the Term "Alaska Native" Using a Definition Similar to that Used in ANCSA as well as in Existing MMPA Regulations; Explore Options for Amending the Definition through the Legislative Process

As noted above, the MMPA does not currently include a definition of the term "Alaska Native" and does not use consistent terminology when referring to Alaska's indigenous people.

MMPA regulations, at 50 C.F.R. § 216.3, do establish a definition of the term "Alaskan Native" that is similar to the definition of the term "Native" under ANCSA. As introduced, the Alaska Native Access Card Act would simply amend the MMPA to incorporate the regulatory definition of "Alaska Native" into the statute, and standardize the use of the term "Alaska Native" throughout the MMPA.

In introducing the Alaska Native Access Card Act, Senator Sullivan's staff indicated that there would need to be a conversation with the broader Alaska Native community about how best to define the term Alaska Native within the MMPA.

(5) Do Not Amend the MMPA to Define the Term "Alaska Native"

Although the MMPA itself does not define "Alaska Native," MMPA regulations, at 50 C.F.R. § 216.3, currently do define the term "Alaskan Native" to mean:

> "a person defined in the Alaska Native Claims Settlement Act (43 U.S.C. 1602(b)) (85 Stat. 588) as a citizen of the United States who is of one-fourth degree or more Alaska Indian (including Tsimishian Indians enrolled or not enrolled in the Metlakatla Indian Community), Eskimo, or Aleut blood or combination thereof. The term includes any Native, as so defined, either or both of whose adoptive parents are not Natives. It also includes, in the absence of proof of a minimum blood quantum, any citizen of the United States who is regarded as an Alaska Native by the Native village or group, of which he claims to be a member and whose father or mother is (or, if deceased, was) regarded as Native by any Native village or Native group. Any such citizen enrolled by the Secretary of the Interior pursuant to section 5 of the Alaska Native Claims Settlement Act shall be conclusively presumed to be an Alaskan Native for purposes of this part."

[1] While the final clause of the definition obviously appears to limit the applicability of the definition only to those tribes that are "recognized as eligible for the special programs and services provided by the United States to Indians because of their status as Indians," the Ninth Circuit in 1987 supported a conclusion that Congress also intended to include Alaska Native corporations notwithstanding the eligibility clause. *See Cook Inlet Native Ass'n v. Bowen*, 810 F.2d 1471 (9th Cir. 1987).

As noted above, the MMPA regulatory definition of the term "Alaskan Native" is similar to the definition of "Native" under Section 3 of ANCSA.

Given current reliance on the MMPA regulatory definition of "Alaskan Native," the Alaska Native Access Card Act does not need to amend the MMPA itself to include the definition within the statute. However, by proposing to add a definition of "Alaska Native" to the MMPA, the bill essentially elevates the question of how best to define the term as part of the legislative process.

APPENDIX 11: FWS TAGGING PACKET FOR WALRUS

DEPARTMENT OF THE INTERIOR
U.S. FISH & WILDLIFE SERVICE
WALRUS CERTIFICATE #

Tagging Date (1)

Tagging Location (2)

Village Hunted From (If Different) (3)

MTRP Tag # (Pairs)	Take Type LK	Take Type BF	Date Killed / Found	Age A	Age SA	Sex M	Sex F	Sex U	Tusk Circ	Tusk Lgth	Location Killed / Found
1 L (4) R (5)	(6)		(7)	(8)		(9)			(10)	(11)	(12)
2 L R											
3 L R											
4 L R											
5 L R											

In addition to the walrus listed above, how many walrus without tusks were harvested: (13)

Calves ______ Yearlings ______ Adults with no tusks ______

Remarks (14)

Signature of Tagger (15)

Name of Hunter (Print) (16)

Signature of Hunter (17)

Instructions on Inside of Front Cover

WHITE-ORIGINAL PINK-HUNTER'S COPY YELLOW-TAGGER'S COPY

Gum Line

Tusk Length

INSTRUCTIONS FOR WALRUS FORM

Tusks from each walrus should be tagged in pairs

1. Record the date tusks are tagged.
2. Village where tusks are tagged.
3. Village walrus was hunted from if different than tagging village.
4. Record tag number of plastic-headed wire tag used for left tusk.
5. Record tag number of plastic-headed wire tag used for right tusk.
6. Take type – mark column that describes how tusks were obtained: LK – live killed, and retrieved the same day; BF – beach found, walrus found dead on the beach. All floaters are to be marked as BF.
7. Record date of kill or beach find as month, day, and year.
8. Age of walrus. A = Adult, male with tusks 12 inches or longer; female with tusks 8 inches or longer. SA = Sub-Adult, male with tusks showing that are less than 12 inches; female with tusks showing that are less than 8 inches.
9. Sex of walrus: M = male; F = female; U = unknown.
10. Measure and record tusk circumference at gum line (see example above).
11. Measure and record tusk length from gum line to tip along front side following the curve of the tusk (see example above).
12. Record exact location of kill or find. For example – 3 miles east of Barrow or 6 miles S.W. of South Cape, St. Lawrence Island. Be specific.
13. Record number of calves, yearlings, and walrus without tusks harvested in addition to the tagged walrus recorded above.
14. Record any information of interest or unusual circumstances about the animal, health or condition of walrus, specimens removed for analysis.
15. The tagger signs here.
16. Print the name of the hunter.
17. The hunter or owner signs here

After completing certificate, give pink copy to hunter, return white copy to our office,
U.S. Fish and Wildlife Service / Marine Mammals Management
Marking, Tagging, and Reporting
1011 East Tudor Road MS341
Anchorage, AK 99503
and retain the yellow copy in book for your records.

OMB Control No. 1018-0066
Expiration Date: 6/30/2017

DEPARTMENT OF THE INTERIOR
U.S. FISH & WILDLIFE SERVICE
WALRUS CERTIFICATE #

Tagging Date ____________

Tagging Location ____________

Village Hunted From (If Different) ____________

MTRP Tag # (Pairs)	Take Type		Date Killed / Found	Age		Sex			Tusk Circ	Tusk Lgth	Location Killed / Found
	LK	BF		A	SA	M	F	U			
1 L											
1 R											
2 L											
2 R											
3 L											
3 R											
4 L											
4 R											
5 L											
5 R											

In addition to the walrus listed above, how many walrus without tusks were harvested:

Calves ______ Yearlings ______ Adults with no tusks ______

Remarks ____________

Signature of Tagger ____________

Name of Hunter (Print) ____________

Signature of Hunter ____________

Instructions on Inside of Front Cover

WHITE-ORIGINAL PINK-HUNTER'S COPY YELLOW-TAGGER'S COPY

APP 3 - 7 - 89

FWS Form 3-2415
7/14

NOTICE

Paperwork Reduction Act and Privacy Act

In accordance with the Paperwork Reduction Act of 1995 (44 U.S.C. 3501, *et seq.*) and the Privacy Act of 1974 (5 U.S.C. 552a), please be advised that:

1. The gathering of information on marine mammals harvested by Alaska Natives is authorized by :
   (a) The Marine Mammal Protection Act of 1972 (16.S.C. 1379(i)); and
   (b) Title 50, Part 18 of the Code of Federal Regulations.

2. Information requested on this form is required to obtain a benefit and comply with statutory and regulatory requirements. This information is being collected to monitor the subsistence harvest of walrus and will be used to obtain essential biological data necessary to manage the species. The collection of this information will also help control the illegal take, trade, and transport of specified raw marine mammal parts. Response is not required unless a currently valid Office of Management and Budget (OMB) control number is displayed.

3. Routine use disclosures may be made:
   (a) To the U.S. Dept. of Justice when related to litigation or anticipated litigation;
   (b) Of information indicating a violation or potential violation of a statute, regulation, rule, order or license to appropriate Federal, State, local or foreign agencies responsible for investigation or prosecuting the violation or for enforcing or implementing the statute, rule, regulation, order or license;
   (c) From the record of an individual in response to an inquiry from a Congressional office made at the request of that individual (42 FR 1903; April 11, 1977)

4. All names will be removed when we compile results, and only summary information will be reported.

5. The relevant burden to report information required on this form and have the specified parts marked or tagged is 15 minutes. Direct comments regarding the burden estimate or any other aspect of the form to Service Information Clearance Officer, U.S. Fish and Wildlife Service, 1849 C Street, NW., (Mailstop BPHC), Washington, D.C. 20240.

Freedom of Information Act

For organization, businesses, or individuals operating as a business (i.e., permittees not covered by the Privacy Act), we request that you identify any information that should be considered privileged and confidential business information to allow the Service to meet its responsibilities under FOIA. Confidential business information must be clearly marked "Business Confidential" at the top of the letter or page and each succeding page and must be accompanied by a non-confidential summary of the confidential information. The non-confidential summary and remaining documents may be made available to the public under FOIA [43 CFR 2.13(c)(4), 43 CFR 2.15(d)(1)(i)].

Application Processing Fee

There is no fee associated with this form.

Made in the USA
Middletown, DE
20 December 2021

56375346R00080